How to Prepare a Research Article in APA Style

Fred Spooner

Bob Algozzine

University of North Carolina at Charlotte

Meagan Karvonen

Western Carolina University

Ya-yu Lo

University of North Carolina at Charlotte

Council for Exceptional Children
2900 Crystal Drive, Suite 1000
Arlington, VA 22202
www.cec.sped.org

Library of Congress Cataloging-in-Publication data

Spooner, Fred.
How to prepare a research article in APA style / by Fred Spooner, Bob Algozzine, Meagan Karvonen and Ya-yu Lo.
p. cm.
Includes biographical references.

ISBN 978-0-86586-458-0 (soft cover edition)
ISBN 978-0-86586-511-2 (eBook edition)

Cover design by Carol Williams.

Layout by Del Moran.

Printed in the United States of America by Sheridan Books.

First edition

10 9 8 7 6 5 4 3 2

Contents

Foreword 5

Abstract 8

Abstract Example: Group Design 9

Abstract Example: Qualitative Design 10

Abstract Example: Single-Case Design... 11

Abstract Example: Position Paper 12

How to Prepare a Research Article in APA Style 13

    Method 14

    Results.. 17

    Discussion 19

    References 20

    Table 1 – Examples From Well-Written Introductions 24

    Table 2 – Examples of Well-Written Participant and Setting Descriptions ... 26

    Table 3 – Examples of Well-Written Method Sections 28

    Table 4 – Male and Female Mathematics and Written Expression
        Achievement Comparisons 34

    Table 5 – Examples of Well-Written Results.. 35

    Table 6 – Examples of Well-Written Discussion.................................. 38

    Figure 1 – Graphic Depiction of the Three Sections of an Introduction....... 40

    Figure 2 – Male and Female Participants' Math and Writing Performance... 41

    Appendix A – A Baker's Dozen Style Tips.. 42

    Appendix B – Review of Key Features of Manuscript Preparation.............. 44

    Appendix C – A Few Rules of the Game 46

    Appendix D – Guidelines for the Use of Seriation and Headings................ 48

    Appendix E – Crediting Sources 52

    Appendix F – Miscellaneous Considerations....................................... 60

    Appendix G – Reviews, Reviewers, Reviewing, and Electronic Manuscript
        Submission and Review Systems.. 62

    Table G-1 – Criteria for Judging Manuscripts: Questions to Ask About
        Research and Presentation 82

    Table G-2 – Questions and Guidelines for Authors to Prepare a Manuscript
        Before Submission 84

    Appendix H – Reporting Research Results 86

    Appendix I – Tips for Moving From the 5th to the 6th Edition.................. 93

Foreword

This guide is not a substitute for the *Publication Manual of the American Psychological Association* published by the American Psychological Association (APA, 2010). That almost 300-page book is an extensive and invaluable resource and copies should be available in colleges, universities, and in the public domain. If you are seriously engaged in disseminating scholarship and research, and brief guides like this one do not suffice, you should purchase a copy of the APA "*Publication Manual*" for professional use (approximately $30 in paperback; see http://www.apastyle.org/manual/index.aspx).

To our knowledge, no other guide on preparing a research article for publication in APA style exists; however, in addition to books, the American Psychological Association makes a variety of resources on APA style available online (see http://apastyle.apa.org/index.aspx):

- http://apastyle.apa.org/learn/tutorials/basics-tutorial.aspx. If you have no prior knowledge of APA style, this tutorial is a great place to start. It illustrates general principles of structure and format, describes important aspects of professional writing, and provides examples of ways to cite the writing of others in your work.

- http://apastyle.apa.org/learn/tutorials/brief-guide.aspx. This tutorial includes a detailed list of new and expanded material in the latest edition of the APA *Publication Manual*.

- http://apastyle.apa.org/manual/whats-new.aspx. This is a brief summary of key changes and a chapter-by-chapter review of what has changed in the new 6th edition of the APA *Publication Manual*.

- http://www.apastyle.org/learn/index.aspx. This is a collection of resources that support learning of APA style.

- http://apastyle.apa.org/manual/supplement/index.aspx. This is a collection of supplementary material that is referenced but not printed in the APA *Publication Manual*.

Other web-based resources with examples of APA format and style are available from the Purdue Online Writing Lab (http://owl.english.purdue.edu/owl/resource/560/01/) and Wake Forest University (http://zsr.wfu.edu/research/guides/apa.html). To assist researchers, faculty, and students, additional guidelines and tips on scholarly writing and publishing are available in an online resource created by the American Educational Research Association (Uchiyama & Kozik-Rosabal, 1999).

A Final Note. With the exception of the Foreword, the format for this guide mimics that of a research article prepared in APA style. The general sections (e.g., Abstract, Introduction, Method, Results) have been formatted consistently with APA expectations. Appendices A to I contain supplementary material including style tips, checkpoints for preparing manuscripts, selected APA rules, guidelines for using headings and formatting references, and other considerations as well as some thoughts on reviews, reviewers, and reviewing associated with publishing empirical research. We hope you enjoy this guide and find it useful.

FS, BA, MK, YL

How to Prepare a Research Article in APA Style

Fred Spooner and Bob Algozzine

University of North Carolina at Charlotte

Meagan Karvonen

Western Carolina University

Ya-yu Lo

University of North Carolina at Charlotte

Author Note

Fred Spooner and Bob Algozzine, College of Education, University of North Carolina at Charlotte; Meagan Karvonen, College of Education, Western Carolina University; Ya-yu Lo, College of Education, University of North Carolina at Charlotte.

Preparation of this manuscript was supported by Grant XTR24A0007845 from the Institute of Funding Sciences, U.S. Department of Education. The opinions expressed herein are those of the authors, and no official endorsement should be inferred.

Correspondence concerning this article should be addressed to Fred Spooner, Special Education/COED, University of North Carolina at Charlotte, Charlotte, NC 28223. E-mail: fhspoone@uncc.edu

---

Note. Try to keep your title to no more than 12 words and avoid phrases such as *A Study of* or *An Investigation of* when informing readers about content and focus of your article. (See pp. 23-25, and 229 of APA *Publication Manual* for more information on preparing a "title" page for your article).

Abstract

The second page (which follows the title page) of your manuscript should be an abstract (i.e., a brief, comprehensive summary of the article, once it is published). It should be a single paragraph in block format (i.e., without paragraph indention) and should contain 150 to 250 words that summarize your work in 4 to 7 sentences; however, we recommend checking submission guidelines of the journal to which you will be submitting your manuscript for recommended word limits. An abstract for a report of an empirical investigation should include a sentence or two describing each of the following: (a) the problem under investigation, (b) the participants and their relevant characteristics, (c) the method, (d) the outcomes and significance levels, and (e) the conclusions and implications reflected in the work. Directly below your abstract, you should list a few keywords of value in abstracting and indexing your article in electronic databases. Your goal should be to provide a summary that is accurate, concise, self-contained, and specific.

Keywords. APA style, professional writing, writing for publication

Note. The next page of your manuscript should begin by repeating the title followed by an "introduction" that puts the purpose of your work and the problem being studied in a context of prior knowledge. We have inserted examples of abstracts because we thought it made sense to provide illustrations immediately after the brief description rather than in a table as we have done with other illustrative material.

(See pp. 25-27 of APA *Publication Manual* for more information on preparing an abstract for your article.)

Abstract Example: Group Design

Although early work experiences during high school represent one of the most consistent predictors of postschool employment for young adults with disabilities, little is known about how these adolescents might access these valuable transition experiences. This study examined the summer employment and community activities of 136 high school students with severe disabilities. The majority of youth was either not working (61.7%) or reported sheltered employment (11.1%). The most prominent predictors of summer employment status were holding a job during the spring semester and teacher expectations for employment. Recommendations for research and practice focus on increasing the capacity of schools, families, and communities to support the involvement of youth with severe disabilities in meaningful summer activities.

Carter, E., Dutchman, N., Ye, S., Trainer, A., Swedeen, B., & Owens, L. (2010). Summer employment and community experiences of transition-age youth with severe disabilities. *Exceptional Children*, *76*, 194-212. Retrieved from Academic Search Premier database.

Why we think it is a good abstract:

- The length (e.g., 115 words) is within style recommendations.

- The topic under consideration is clearly evident (i.e., predictors of postschool employment and how adolescents access transition experiences).

- The participants and procedures are delimited (i.e., analysis of summer employment and community activities of high school students with severe disabilities).

- The outcomes are summarized (e.g., most prominent predictors were holding a job during the spring semester and teacher expectations for employment).

Abstract Example: Qualitative Design

This article examined self-definition in a sample of adolescents with and without disabilities to understand how they develop a sense of themselves and influential contextual factors. Central findings focus attention on students' self-definition, the degree to which they struggle in their lives, and the social support they are able to access and use. Students varied on level of self-definition, struggle, and type of support. Variation was dependent upon the clarity of the students' sense of themselves, their vision for the future, and their access to and use of supports to cope with decisions and difficulties faced as they prepared to graduate from high school. Students with disabilities were most likely to have low self-definition and experience high struggle.

Whitney-Thomas, J., & Moloney, M. (2001). "Who I am and what I want": Adolescents' self-definition and struggles. *Exceptional Children, 67,* 375-389.

Why we think it is a good abstract:

- The length (e.g., 118 words) is within style recommendations.

- The topic under consideration is clearly noted (i.e., self-definition in adolescents).

- The participants and method are evident (i.e., self-definitions and other aspects of adolescents' lives were documented and analyzed).

- The outcomes are reflected (e.g., individuals varied on self-definition and variation was related to individual factors).

Abstract Example: Single-Case Design

A multiple probe across participants design assessed the effectiveness of an instructional strategy to teach 10 elementary-aged students with moderate intellectual disabilities how to shop for grocery items. Following the intervention, which consisted of *in vivo* training using constant time delay and simulation training using a pictorial storyboard, 6 students achieved criterion. Two other students' shopping performances improved considerably during training, but the students did not achieve criterion as training was discontinued due to the end of the school year. Maintenance data indicate that the students who achieved criterion retained their skills for 6 weeks, and generalization data indicate that they could shop for the same items in a novel store.

Morse, T. E., & Schuster, J. W. (2000). Teaching elementary students with moderate intellectual disabilities how to shop for groceries. *Exceptional Children, 66,* 273-288.

Why we think it is a good abstract:

- The length (e.g., 111 words) is within style recommendations.

- The type and number of participants (10 elementary-aged students with moderate intellectual disabilities) are delimited.

- The experimental design (i.e., multiple probe across participants) is evident.

- The intervention (e.g., how to shop for grocery items) and the training procedures are presented.

- The outcomes (e.g., 6 students achieved criterion) as well as generalization and maintenance data are reported.

Abstract Example: Position Paper

An overview of the many types of studies that fall into the qualitative design genre is provided. Strategies that qualitative researchers use to establish the authors' studies as credible and trustworthy are listed and defined. So that readers will recognize the important contribution qualitative studies have made in the field of special education, a range of well-known and lesser known examples of qualitative research are reviewed. The quality indicators that are important in conducting and evaluating qualitative research are identified. Finally, as an example of the evidence that can be produced using qualitative methods, the authors provide a summary of how 3 studies have provided important information that can be used to inform policy and practice.

Brantlinger, E., Jimenez, R., Klingner, J., Pugach, M., & Richardson, V. (2005). Qualitative studies in special education. *Exceptional Children, 71,* 195-207.

Why we think it is a good abstract:

- The length (e.g., 116 words) is within style recommendations.

- The topic being addressed is clearly evident (i.e., overview of types of qualitative studies).

- The content and focus is delimited (i.e., strategies used by qualitative researchers, examples of qualitative research, indicators of value in conducting and evaluating qualitative research).

- The implications are evident (e.g., information that can be used to inform policy and practice is evident).

How to Prepare a Research Article in APA Style

A research article is one in which a question or series of questions derived from a body of literature is addressed by the collection of original data which are subsequently used to provide answers that can be generalized with appropriate limitations and restrictions. In most research articles, the *introduction* is brief (2-3 pages); the section describing the *method* is somewhat longer (3-5 pages); *results* are presented succinctly and, depending on the complexity of the study, may be brief or long (3-5 pages) and may be supplemented by *tables* or *figures*; and, the *discussion* of what it all means is usually substantial (5-7 pages), with emphasis on linking the work to extant literature and bringing the implications of the work forward for improving the knowledge base and professional practice. The content, emphasis, and length of each section will vary with the thrust of the article and the audience as well as the nature of the study.

The introduction to the article should make the purpose, worth, and need for the research immediately clear; that is, it should describe what is known about the topic under investigation, why the study was necessary, what was intended to be accomplished, and why the outcomes are important. The introduction is usually a review of literature describing the need, purpose, and importance of the study. Typically, an introduction will contain three sections. The first section is a broad stroke, general treatment of the topic under consideration. The second section is a synthesis of relevant literature used to establish what is known about the topic under investigation and to establish a specific need for the research. The third section is a more highly focused amplification that clearly describes the purpose of the study (see Figure 1).

Articles based on dissertation research often require the most editing in the introduction and literature review. Sometimes, however, if the dissertation began with a brief introduction putting the problem in context and concluding with a statement of purpose or overview of methods, that section may be used almost as is for the introduction of the article.

Any literature cited in the introduction (or other parts of the article) must be included in the reference section. A common practice in preparing this section of the article is to use several paragraphs to discuss other studies pointing to different opinions or raising questions that have been answered in the study.

To summarize, the introduction of the article (a) describes the problem, (b) develops the background, and (c) provides a clear indication of the purpose and rationale for the study. Table 1 provides examples of sections from well-written introductions. A good introduction answers the following questions and gives the reader a firm sense of what was done and why (APA, 2010, p. 27):

- Why is this problem important?

- How do the hypothesis and the experimental design relate to the problem?

- What are the theoretical implications of the study, and how does the study relate to previous work in the area?

- What theoretical propositions are tested, and how were they derived?

Method

The Method section describes in detail how the study was conducted (cf. APA, 2010, pp. 29-32). Begin with a one- or two-sentence overview of the method that was used to conduct the study. A list of hypotheses or a sentence description of the purpose and objectives can also be used to introduce the method before formally describing what was done in the study.

The description should provide the reader with sufficient information to evaluate the appropriateness and integrity of what was done as well as the reliability and validity of the outcomes derived from doing it. This section should also provide enough detail for other investigators to replicate the study if they so desire.

The Method section is typically divided into labeled subsections. These sections usually include a description of the *participants and setting* and the *procedures*, including an explanation of the instruments or measures as well as design and data analysis procedures. Again, the purpose is to provide information essential for others to comprehend and replicate the study.

Insufficient detail leaves the reader with questions; too much detail burdens the reader with irrelevant information. We describe each of these components in greater detail in the following subsections.

Participants and Setting

Sample characteristics and information on the setting for the study should be provided early in the Method section. The goal here is to set the context for the research, including information about selection criteria, demographics, and location of the study. For studies following a group design, use numbers to reflect group representation, if appropriate, and whenever possible indicate the sample's representativeness with regard to the population under investigation. For a single-case research study (applied behavior analysis), describe the participant(s), listing parameters such as age, characteristics, IQ, and limitations and strengths. Qualitative studies, with participants ranging from a single individual in a case study to an entire cultural group in an ethnographic study, use a variety of methods to describe the participants. When possible, individual participant characteristics should be described much like those in a single-subject study, with attention to characteristics that are especially relevant to the research questions. If a larger entity (e.g., a school system) is the focus of the study, descriptive characteristics about that organization should be included. In general, this section helps the reader understand who participated and sets the parameters for generalization of the obtained outcomes. Table 2 provides examples of well-written participant and setting descriptions.

Procedure

This subsection is used to summarize important aspects of the research methods, including what was done to address the research questions of interest (see Table 3). The description should be of sufficient detail to warrant confidence about what was done and to help others in conducting similar work. Qualitative researchers may wish to place additional emphasis on the rationale for their approach, especially if it includes methods that might be unfamiliar to the audience. If appropriate and necessary, consider dividing this section into subsections for detailed descriptions of the intervention and instrumentation (and apparatus) as well as design and data analysis.

Intervention. If the study involved implementation of a treatment or program, it should be described. If what mattered most about the study was not the intervention but the assessment of its effect, do not spend a lot of space describing what was done. If, however, the focus of the research was testing a new or complex intervention, then describe it extensively so others can replicate or use it. This rule of thumb applies to both quantitative and qualitative studies. The focus of an applied behavior analytic study should be a detailed description of the intervention to the extent that another researcher, with interest in the same topical area, could read the account of the intervention that you have written and replicate or reproduce the procedure(s).

Instrumentation. Describe measurement tools used for data collection and their technical adequacy in a subsection if warranted by their importance to the study. Physiological measurements are typically described first, followed by observations and questionnaires or interviews, thus moving from more objective and precise data to more subjective and imprecise information. Provide an indication of the acceptability and previous use of all measures, relying on earlier research and established technical adequacy data (e.g., validity and reliability) to support use whenever possible. Describe the rationale, development procedures, and technical characteristics of any measures produced specifically for the study. If appropriate, describe any special apparatus or materials used in the study as well as their function with regard to the outcomes. The use of recording devices (e.g., videotape recorders) in qualitative studies should also be noted if used to ensure the accuracy of data. The main thing to remember is that the description of the instrumentation should prepare the reader for the findings that will be discussed in the Results section and establish confidence in them.

In survey research, this section often describes procedures used in developing the questionnaire or survey. Numbers and content of items as well as technical considerations are typically described in sufficient detail to support adoption, adaptation, or application by others. In applied behavior analytic research in the area of skill training for persons with disabilities, this section might require the description of the task analysis that was used to teach the skill.

Some additional considerations are warranted for those writing about qualitative research. Because qualitative studies often employ nonstandardized instruments (e.g., focus group interviews) designed specifically for the current study, the instrument content (e.g., open-ended questions), development process (e.g., pilot testing), and format (e.g., semistructured interview) should also be described in some detail. The role of the researcher in relationship to the study participants (e.g., participant observer) should also be noted.

Design and data analysis. Thesis writers frequently explain the technical operations they employed to organize and analyze their data in detail, sometimes even naming the statistical package used to arrange, compile, and conduct statistical analyses and significance tests. In a journal article, the researcher(s) understand the design and statistics that were used and have dealt appropriately with their research questions, hypotheses, and data. Design and data analysis information is generally included only when this aspect of the study needs clarification to support replication. Thus researchers employing group designs often simply inform the reader how participants were assigned to groups (e.g., randomly) and label the design (e.g., split-plot factorial). In this subsection, the applied behavior analytic researcher would delineate the experimental design (e.g., multiple baseline across participants) that was used in the study, and explain the type of analysis (e.g., visual inspection) that was employed to examine the potential effects of the intervention. Qualitative studies should include a summary of the data collection schedule, as well as descriptions of the data coding process, identification of themes, and the approach(es) used in data analysis (e.g., grounded theory).

Results

The Results section is used to summarize the data collected and the statistical treatment of them in support of the research questions addressed in the study (see APA, 2010, pp. 32-35). The main outcomes are typically presented first, with sufficient detail to justify conclusions with regard to underlying and organizing hypotheses. All relevant results, statistically significant ones as well as those that are not significant, should be addressed, including those that run counter to preconceived questions. For a single-case experimental design study, the investigator refers the reader to the charted data, usually presented in a figure, and describes in the text the effects including the mean and range of baseline performance, for all participants, one at a time, and the shift in performance during the intervention phase of the study, again specifying the mean and the range. The results obtained from qualitative studies vary widely according to the data collected and the analytic method used; as a result, there is generally greater flexibility in the manner in which qualitative results are reported (cf. McWilliam, 2000). The Results section should include identification of common or emergent themes, exceptions to the primary findings, and unexpected outcomes. Data collected qualitatively and summarized quantitatively should also be summarized here. Most findings are reported within the text and may be supported with direct quotations from participants or examples that support the findings. However, some data may be best reported graphically (e.g., in a causal flowchart).

Tables and figures. Most journals rarely have space for more than two or three tables or figures in an article. Before you include a table or figure, try to decide if it contains vital information that helps to organize the presentation of findings. Tables provide exact values and efficiently illustrate outcomes; for example, means, standard deviations, and obtained *t* statistics for achievement scores for male and female participants might be presented in tabular form to depict an important comparison and its outcomes (see Table 4). Figures, such as charts and pictures, attract the reader's eye and are also used to illustrate outcomes; but, they are usually not as precise as tables (see Figure 2). Figures may tend to be more valuable in qualitative studies, where a detailed analysis of a social phenomenon, for example, might yield information that cannot be adequately conveyed in tabular form (e.g., causal model, social map).

Summarizing analyses and results in tables and figures instead of text can be very helpful, especially when large amounts of data are reduced by representation in a form other than sentences in paragraphs; however, using tables or figures for data that can easily be presented in a few sentences of text is not a good idea. Tables and figures should augment rather than duplicate text, conveying essential facts without distracting details. The goal is to achieve a parsimonious balance in presenting the outcomes of the study (see Table 5 for references to single-case, quantitative, and qualitative examples). If you use tables and figures in your article, be sure to mention all of them in the text. Refer to all tables as *tables* and all charts, graphs, photographs, drawings, or other depictions as *figures*. Tables and figures supplement the text; they do not stand alone. Always tell the reader what to look for in the tables and figures and provide sufficient explanation to make the presentation easily comprehensible. Extensive information is available in other sources on preparing and using tables and figures in reporting research findings (cf. APA, 2010, pp. 125-167).

Discussion

The Discussion section ties the outcomes of the research to the literature and takes readers beyond the facts to the meaning they reflect, the questions they raise, the ideas to which they point, and the practical uses and value they have for the extension of knowledge (see Table 6 for examples). Consider opening the discussion with a clear statement relating the findings to the original questions or hypotheses. Similarities and differences between the study's outcomes and the work of others also are useful beginnings for the final section of the article. Be careful, however, not to simply reformulate, rehash, and repeat points made earlier in the article. Statements in the discussion should contribute to a position and the reader's understanding of the problem. Finally, do not overemphasize limitations and do not generalize beyond the outcomes of the study; speculation is acceptable if it is (a) identified as such, (b) related closely and logically to key aspects of the study, and (c) expressed in reasonable and concise form.

References

American Psychological Association. (2010). *Publication manual of the American Psychological Association* (6th ed.). Washington, DC: Author.

Ayvazoglu, N. R., Oh, H.-K., & Kozub, F. M. (2006). Explaining physical activity in children with visual impairments: A family systems approach. *Exceptional Children, 72*, 235-248.

Barton-Arwood, S. M., Wehby, J. H., & Falk, K. B. (2005). Reading instruction for elementary-age students with emotional and behavioral disorders: Academic and behavioral outcomes. *Exceptional Children, 72*, 7-27.

Brantlinger, E., Jimenez, R., Klingner, J., Pugach, M., & Richardson, V. (2005). Qualitative studies in special education. *Exceptional Children, 71*, 195-207.

Browder, D. M., & Minarovic, T. J. (2000). Utilizing sight words in self-instruction training for employees with moderate mental retardation in competitive jobs. *Education and Training in Mental Retardation and Developmental Disabilities, 35*, 78-89.

Brownell, M. T., Adams, A., Sindelar, P., Waldron, N., & Vanhover, S. (2006). Learning from collaboration: The role of teacher qualities. *Exceptional Children, 72*, 169-185.

Brownell, M. T., Bishop, A. G., Gersten, R., Klingner, J. K., Penfield, R. D., Dimino, J.,... Sindelar, P. T. (2009). The role of domain expertise in beginning special education teacher quality. *Exceptional Children, 75*, 391-411.

Browning, P., & Nave, G. (1993). Teaching social problem solving to learners with mild disabilities. *Education and Training in Mental Retardation and Developmental Disabilities, 28*, 309-317.

Carter, E., Dutchman, N., Ye, S., Trainer, A., Swedeen, B., & Owens, L. (2010). Summer employment and community experiences of transition-age youth with severe disabilities. *Exceptional Children, 76*, 194-212.

Causton-Theoharis, J. N., & Malmgren, K. W. (2005). Increasing peer interactions for students with severe disabilities via paraprofessional training. *Exceptional Children, 71*, 431-444.

Cunningham, A. E., & Stanovich, K. E. (1997). Early reading acquisition and its relation to reading experience and ability 10 years later. *Developmental Psychology, 33*, 934-945.

Daly, T. C., & Carlson, E. (2009). Predictors of change in eligibility status among preschoolers in special education. *Exceptional Children, 75*, 412-426.

Gersten, R., Baker, S. K., Smith-Johnson, J., Dimino, J., & Peterson, A. (2006). Eyes on the prize: Teaching complex historical content to middle school students with learning disabilities. *Exceptional Children, 72*, 264-280.

Hundert, J., & Hopkins, B. (1992). Training supervisors in a collaborative team approach to promote peer interaction of children with disabilities in integrated preschools. *Journal of Applied Behavior Analysis, 25*, 385-400.

Kozub, F. M. (2003). Explaining physical activity in individuals with mental retardation: An exploratory study. *Education and Training in Developmental Disabilities, 38*, 302-313.

Kozub, F. M., & Oh, H. (2004). An exploratory study of physical activity levels in children and adolescents with visual impairments. *Clinical Kinesiology, 58*(3), 1-7.

Lane, K. L., Givner, C. C., & Pierson, M. R. (2004). Teacher expectations of student behavior: Social skills necessary for success in elementary school classrooms. *The Journal of Special Education, 38*, 104-110.

Lane, K. L., Little, M. A., Redding-Rhodes, J., Phillips, A., & Welsh, M. T. (2007). Outcomes of a teacher-led reading intervention for elementary students at risk for behavioral disorders. *Exceptional Children, 74*, 47-70.

Lane, K. L., Wehby, J. H., & Cooley, C. (2006). Teacher expectations of students' classroom behavior across the grade span: Which social skills are necessary for success? *Exceptional Children, 72,* 153-167.

Leppänen, U., Aunola, K., & Nurmi, J. E. (2005). Beginning readers' reading performance and reading habits. *Journal of Research in Reading, 28,* 383-399.

Lynch, S., Taymans, J., Watson, W. A., Ochsendorf, R. J., Pyke, C., & Szesze, M. J. (2007). Effectiveness of a highly rated science curriculum unit for students with disabilities in general education classrooms. *Exceptional Children, 73,* 202-223.

Martin, J. E., Van Dycke, J. L., Greene, B. A., Gardner, J. E., Christensen, W. R., Woods, L. L., & Lovett, D. L. (2006). Direct observation of teacher-directed IEP meetings: Establishing the need for student IEP meeting instruction. *Exceptional Children, 72,* 187-200.

McWilliam, R. A. (2000). Reporting qualitative studies. *Journal of Early Intervention, 23,* 77-80.

Morgan, P. L., & Fuchs, D. (2007). Is there a bidirectional relationship between children's reading skills and reading motivation? *Exceptional Children, 73,* 165-183.

Morse, T. E., & Schuster, J. W. (2000). Teaching elementary students with moderate intellectual disabilities how to shop for groceries. *Exceptional Children, 66,* 273-288.

Nelson, J. R., Duppong Hurley, K., Synhorst, L., Epstein, M. H., Stage, S., & Buckley, J. (2009). The child outcomes of a behavior model. *Exceptional Children, 76,* 7-30.

Purcell, M. L., Horn, E., & Palmer, S. (2007). A qualitative study of the initiation and continuation of preschool inclusion programs. *Exceptional Children, 74,* 85-99.

Rueda, R., Monzo, L., Shapiro, J., Gomez, J., & Blacher, J. (2005). Cultural models of transition: Latina mothers of young adults with developmental disabilities. *Exceptional Children, 71*, 401-414.

Shapiro, J., Monzo, L., Rueda, R., Gomez, J., & Blacher, J. (2004). Alienated advocacy: The perspective of Latina mothers of young adults with developmental disabilities on service systems. *Mental Retardation, 42*, 37-54.

Sindelar, P. T., Shearer, D. K., Yendol-Hoppey, D., & Liebert, T. W. (2006). The sustainability of inclusive school reform. *Exceptional Children, 72*, 317-331.

Tabachnick, B., & Fidell, L. (1989). *Using multivariate statistics* (3rd ed.). New York, NY: HarperCollins College.

Tawney, J. W., & Gast, D. L. (1984). *Single subject research in special education*. Columbus, OH: Merrill.

Uchiyama, K., & Kozik-Rosabal, G. (1999). *Publishing educational research: Guidelines and tips*. Washington, DC: American Educational Research Association (Under the mentorship of Hilda Borko) Available online: http://www.aera.net/epubs/index.htm

Vaughn, S., Schumm, J. S., & Sinagub, J. (1996). *Focus group interviews in education and psychology*. Thousand Oaks, CA: Sage.

Whitney-Thomas, J., & Moloney, M. (2001). "Who I am and what I want": Adolescents' self-definition and struggles. *Exceptional Children, 67*, 375-389.

Will, M. C. (1986). Educating students with learning problems: A shared responsibility. *Exceptional Children, 52*, 411-415.

Table 1
Examples From Well-Written Introductions

Element	Example
Importance of the Problem	The idea of including students with disabilities in general education classrooms is nearly 30 years old. In 1975, the Individuals with Disabilities Education Act (IDEA) introduced the concept of instructing students in the least restrictive environment (LRE), and for many students with disabilities, the LRE is a general education classroom. A decade later, Will's (1986) call for shared responsibility in educating students with disabilities set schools and researchers on a quest for successful models of inclusion. Despite the growing body of knowledge about school reform and special education practices, researchers know little about the extent to which innovations are sustained over time and what factors influence their sustainability. In short, empirical research on sustainability factors is limited… (cf. Sindelar, Shearer, Yendol-Hoppey, & Liebert, 2006).
Development of Background	…Scholars and others have recommended that schools use three-tier behavior model as an alternative to the implementation of isolated interventions.…Such models are an attractive prevention-oriented alternative to the approach of trying a wide range of isolated interventions to ameliorate the behavioral challenge of children with or at risk of EBD. Within the public and behavioral health fields, three-tier behavior models are conceptualized differently.…In the public health field the three tiers are categorized as primary, secondary, and tertiary.…In the behavioral health field, three-tier behavior models are correlated directly with levels of risk in target populations…Although the public and behavioral health models are both focused on prevention and are effective for systematically organizing and implementing tiers of interventions, the behavioral health model aligns more directly with the universal, selected, and indicated interventions we used to operationalize our three-tier behavioral model.… Three-tier behavioral models such as the one studied here are expected to achieve a range of important child outcomes… (cf. Nelson et al., 2009).
Description of Relevant Scholarship	Children who read frequently grow to become skillful readers.…Frequent reading contributes to growth in sight word recognition, vocabulary, verbal fluency, reading comprehension, and general knowledge.…For example, Leppänen et al. reported a path coefficient of .13 between children's book reading frequency in first grade and their word recognition skills in second grade. Cunningham and Stanovich (1997) found that reading practice accounted for 34% of the variance in 11th graders' vocabulary scores after their 1st grade vocabulary, nonverbal IQ, and comprehension skills were statistically controlled… (cf. Morgan & Fuchs, 2007).

Element	Example
Purpose and Hypotheses– Single Subject	This study investigates the effectiveness of a training program aimed at teaching four paraprofessionals to facilitate interactions between students with severe disabilities and their peers. The research questions under investigation were as follows: Does training of paraprofessionals to facilitate interactions between students with and without disabilities increase the facilitative behavior of the paraprofessionals? More important, does training of paraprofessionals increase the quantity of interactions that occur between students with disabilities and their peers? We predicted that paraprofessional training would positively influence both the behaviors of paraprofessionals and the interactions of students. Based on the findings from other researchers (e.g., Hundert & Hopkins, 1992), we further predicted that gains in facilitative behavior of paraprofessionals would level off at a lower point than gains in peer interaction, given that the goal of facilitative behavior is to encourage independent interactions that blossom into even more interactions as students create meaningful relationships with their peers. (cf. Causton-Theoharis & Malmgren, 2005)
Purpose and Hypotheses– Group Quantitative	We believed that students with LD could learn history if (a) instruction included comprehensible and accessible materials (rather than sole reliance on traditional textbooks), and (b) incorporated instructional delivery strategies that provided numerous opportunities for students to interact with peers and the teacher during the lesson (rather than heavy reliance on lectures and whole class discussions)....Our goal was for students to learn key events, the meaning of these events within a historical period, and to begin to understand the greater significance of those events in contemporary society....We decided that using a traditional control group (i.e., a group taught the same content but using traditional texts and teaching methods) would not make sense since we knew that virtually none of the LD students could read a grade-appropriate text. We therefore set up a more stringent comparison condition....Thus, the randomized controlled trials did not evaluate the curriculum per se, but evaluated whether delivering that content in these specific ways increased learning in inclusive settings. (cf. Gersten, Baker, Smith-Johnson, Dimino, & Peterson, 2006)
Purpose and Rationale- Qualitative	The investigation used an extensive interview process to study how preschool programs addressed a variety of challenges to provide inclusion. The use of a qualitative, multiple embedded-case study design allowed a purposeful selection of sites for use in the study which enabled identification of sites having particularly unique characteristics. This design supported the collection of multiple sources of data related to the goals of the study, examination of a complex process (with many related components), and the development of informative case-descriptive reports to highlight and examine some of the unique challenges that these sites overcame to initiate and continue their inclusive programs. (cf. Purcell, Horn, & Palmer, 2007)

Table 2
Examples of Well-Written Participant and Setting Descriptions

Element	Example
Participants	The PEELS, sponsored by the National Center for Special Education Research in the U.S. Department of Education, is following a nationally representative sample of 3,104 children from a population of approximately 670,000 children who were receiving special education services in 2004, when they were 3 through 5 years old. PEELS used a two-stage sample design: In the first stage, a national sample of local education agencies (LEAs) was selected. In the second stage, a sample of preschoolers with disabilities was selected from lists of eligible children provided by the participating LEAs....Because the PEELS sample was selected by age, not by grade, some of the children were in kindergarten; others were in preschool, day care, or at home. The children may or may not have received early intervention services from birth to age 3 through Part C of IDEA. Eligibility criteria for study participation were....Eighty-eight percent of the families were found eligible for the study, and 80% of those eligible agreed to participate. The data presented have been weighted to generate national estimates. Different weights were used, depending on the sources of data. These weights adjust the child base weights to account for nonresponse on specific data collections in specific waves or groups of waves (cf. Daly & Carlson, 2009).
	The participants were 7 first-grade Caucasian students (3 girls and 4 boys) identified as at risk for behavioral and reading difficulties. Their ages ranged from 6.1 to 7.7 years, with a mean age of 6.96 (SD = 0.66). Two students, Haley and James, had intellectual functioning that was slightly below average....The remaining students scored in the average intellectual range. None of the students were receiving special education services nor did they have any diagnosed disorders....However, six of the students received additional support from the reading specialists at their school during the entire study.[Explanation accompanied by a table summarizing demographic variables, scores on standardized intelligence and social skills tests, and treatment data] (cf. Lane, Little, Redding-Rhodes, Phillips, & Welsh, 2007)

Element	Example
Setting	Sixty-three percent of our 30 schools were classified as high-poverty urban or rural schools. Service delivery models varied between resource (n = 28), self-contained classes (n = 3), and co-teaching or inclusive (n = 3). Instructional time in special education for reading ranged from 120 min a week to 550 min a week. In 44% of the settings, students received additional reading instruction in general education classrooms, except for Florida, where 17 of 18 special education teachers were the sole reading instructors. Teachers delivered instruction in groups ranging from 2 to 16 students. Curriculum ranged from teachers using evidence-based core reading programs…to other teachers using a less prescribed delivery model… (cf. Brownell et al., 2009).
	We selected two elementary schools with principals who were recommended as capable leaders. The teachers at both schools agreed to participate in the project. Hidden View Elementary and Hilton Elementary were 2 of 200 elementary schools in the city where the study was located. Hidden View Elementary, a regular education initiative school, had a student population of 570 students, of which 43.2% were minority and 54.9% received free or reduced-price lunch. All children with mild disabilities were fully included in general education classrooms…(cf. Brownell, Adams, Sindelar, Waldron, & Vanhover, 2006).

Table 3
Examples of Well-Written Method Sections

Element	Example
Intervention	The major purpose of the curriculum is to teach a set of logical steps that are applicable for solving any problem. A total of 33 video scenarios and 65 slides are used in five lessons to depict three problem areas (work-related, people-related, and money-related). The same step-by-step process is used in solving each of them. The curriculum consists of 30 "learning points" that are the guidelines or rules to be taught to the students. Each of the five lessons requires approximately one class period even though they may vary due to a number of factors under the teacher's discretion. The curriculum's instructional design is based upon a multiple instructional or cognitive behavior modification approach....The curriculum's primary mode of delivery is through interactive video....Finally, all students received the curriculum through group instruction so that students could aid each other in discussion, decision making, and role playing. Thus, the interactive-video curriculum was designed to give teachers a direct and significant role. For example, the teachers were able to decide, to some extent, the branching to be followed by the computer, how many and which response options were selected for each problem situation, and whether to proceed to the next problem or repeat the previous one. Teacher control such as this allows for curriculum adaptation to students of various needs and ages. (cf. Browning & Nave, 1993).

Element	Example
	The intervention included a twofold treatment package. In the first phase, the researchers taught the employee to read the sight words that comprised the printed job routine checklist to be used for self-management. In the second phase, the participant learned a self-management strategy. The self-management strategy consisted of two primary components: (a) a verbalized "Did-Next-Show" self-instruction technique; and (b) a self-monitoring technique. *Sight Word Instruction.* At the beginning of each tutorial session (after the first intervention session), the trainer conducted the sight word probe as described under "Dependent Variables." Immediately following this probe, the participant was taught to read the target words that would comprise the self-management checklist. A progressive time delay procedure with a verbal model prompt was used. The progressive delay schedule was applied within each training session. During each tutorial, participants received two trials for each of their five sight words at each delay level. The delay levels moved from a zero to 8-second delay in increments of two seconds. For the first two trials, the trainer presented each flash card and gave an immediate model of the correct response (zero time delay). Correct repetitions were praised. If the repetition was incorrect, the trainer restated the correct word and moved on to the next flash card. On the next two trials, the researcher presented each word, but delayed modeling the answer for 2 seconds. Then on the next two trials, the delay was 4 seconds followed by 6 and 8 seconds with a total of 10 trials of reading each individual word. When the learner independently read a word for two consecutive times prior to the model, the word was no longer presented for the remainder of that session. In addition, words read independently on two prior sight word probes were not trained in the session. Thus, by the end of the session, only the unlearned words were being presented... (cf. Browder & Minarovic, 2000)

Table 3 (Continued)
Examples of Well-Written Method Sections

Element	Example
Instrumentation (physiological measures)	Triaxial accelerometers have been used to study physical activity in children with mental retardation and visual impairments (Kozub, 2003; Kozub & Oh, 2004). Information about participants' height, weight, and age was used to initialize the monitors prior to data collection. Participants (children with visual impairments, siblings, and parents) were asked to wear activity monitors on their right hip for a 1-week period during waking hours. Participants were allowed to remove monitors for sleeping or any activities where immersion in water could potentially damage accelerometers (such as showering or swimming). Researchers called households during the week and reminded participants to wear monitors and checked to make sure monitors were functioning properly. Physical activity scores included the number of minutes that an individual was involved in bouts of moderate to vigorous physical activity (MVPA)... (cf. Ayvazoglu, Oh, & Kozub, 2006).
Instrumentation (survey design)	A modified version of the Teacher Expectations for School Success questionnaire (see Lane, Givner, et al., 2004) was used in this investigation. The questionnaire contained two sections: social skills items and teacher demographic information. The social skills section contained 30 social skills items from the Social Skills Rating System...The 30 items are equally distributed across three factor analytically derived domains: cooperation (e.g., uses time appropriately while waiting for help), assertion (e.g., joins ongoing activity or group without being told to do so), and self-control (e.g., controls temper in conflict situation with peers). The SSRS has strong psychometric properties with coefficient alpha reliabilities ranging from 0.85 to 0.94 across the three social skill domains... Teachers rated the importance of each skill as it related to student success in their classrooms...The importance items of the elementary and secondary versions were factor analyzed separately using the principal axis method to extract factors, followed by a promax (oblique) rotation. Squared multiple correlations served as prior communality estimates... (cf. Lane, Wehby, & Cooley, 2006).

Element	Example
Instrumentation (observation data)	We used 10-second momentary time sampling to determine the percentage of intervals that the IEP team members talked during IEP transition meetings. At the meetings, trained observers received a tape-recorded 10-s beep prompt via their earphones. They then recorded on data collection sheets which IEP team member was talking at the beep prompt. An IEP participant was identified as talking if he or she spoke a word at the prerecorded beep. If multiple people talked at the beep, we recorded this as multiple conversations. When no one talked at the beep, we considered this as no talking. At the start of the meeting observers described the observational process and, when asked, played the recorded tape so the meeting participants could hear the beeps. [Followed by a section describing interobserver agreement.] (cf. Martin et al., 2006).
Instrumentation (qualitative)	Focus groups involve informal discussion among a small group of participants who are asked to express their viewpoints or opinions on a particular topic about which they have special expertise or life experience....The research team used a question protocol (Shapiro et al., 2004) translated by a Latina member of the team who was familiar with the local community, and this translation was then reviewed by other bilingual team members....A familiar and comfortable setting was sought for the meetings, and a back room in a local church was identified by the community agency that assisted in recruiting participants. Focus groups were conducted approximately 2 weeks apart. Each one was about 3 hours in duration. Three focus groups were conducted. The first group included 4 participants and was conducted bilingually, with much code switching....(cf. Rueda, Monzo, Shapiro, Gomez, & Blacher, 2005).

Table 3 (Continued)
Examples of Well-Written Method Sections

Element	Example
Design and data analysis	Analysis of covariance (ANCOVA), with the student as the unit of statistical analysis, was used to generate statistics to address the research questions. Because schools are the sampling unit and students are the unit of statistical analysis for the study, a nesting of students within classrooms by teacher and school was created. However, ANCOVA was selected for data analysis because of the nature of the research questions, the naturalistic quasi-experimental design, and the robustness and familiarity of analysis of variance statistics…research question 1 required a one-way ANCOVA and research question 2 required five two-way ANCOVAs, all with COMA pretest scores as the covariate. Assumptions for these analyses were evaluated using the guideline established in the ANCOVA literature (cf. Tabachnick & Fidell, 1989). The data did not violate any assumptions of normality, linearity, multicolinearity, or singularity, and homogeneity of variance was found to be acceptable. When significant main effects and interactions were found, exploratory follow-up contrasts were conducted to explain the effects. All ANCOVA analyses were performed using SPSS for Windows, Version 12. Effect sizes were calculated for each subgroup for all dependent variables by subtracting the adjusted mean outcome score for the comparison condition from the adjusted mean outcome score for the treatment condition and dividing the difference by the study sample standard deviation… (cf. Lynch et al., 2007).
	This study used a multiple baseline design across subjects (Tawney & Gast, 1984) to determine the effects of the reading intervention. Because reading fluency is critical for reading success…the decision to end baseline and begin the intervention for each student pair was based upon establishing stability (i.e., negative, neutral, or slightly positive trends) in baseline for the oral reading fluency probe data. Baseline and intervention conditions occurred across 27 weeks throughout an academic school year from September to May… (cf. Barton-Arwood, Wehby, & Falk, 2005).

Element	Example
	Data analysis took place simultaneously with data collection. Debriefing sessions were held after each focus group session to begin to identify categories and themes in the data. In addition, written transcripts were reviewed several times by all investigators. Transcript data were compared both within and across groups. Initial ideas, themes, and categories were first identified using open coding (Vaughn, Schumm, & Sinagub, 1996), then fractured and recoded using axial coding to make connections between categories and subcategories that reflected more generalized themes and patterns. Finally, themes were used to form a grounded theory (selective coding) that clarified concepts and allowed for interpretations and conclusions...The goal of analysis was to identify patterns, make comparisons, and contrast one set of data with another in order to explore the cultural models and issues surrounding transitions for these Latina mothers (cf. Rueda, Monzo, Shapiro, Gomez, & Blacher, 2005).

Table 4
Male and Female Mathematics and Written Expression Achievement Comparisons

Achievement	Males		Females		
	M	*SD*	*M*	*SD*	*t* statistic
Mathematics	117.72	17.57	95.83	12.63	3.71*
Written Expression	120.83	15.88	92.83	17.97	4.49*

*$p < 0.05$

Table 5
Examples of Well-Written Results

Citation	Explanation
1. Well-written results include a summary of the statistical treatment of data when appropriate.	
Barton-Arwood, S. M., Wehby, J. H., & Falk, K. B. (2005). Reading instruction for elementary-age students with emotional and behavioral disorders: Academic and behavioral outcomes. *Exceptional Children, 72,* 7-27.	Barton-Arwood, Wehby, and Falk (2005) provided an excellent presentation of single-case research results. The authors reported descriptive statistics (experimental condition means, standard deviations, and slopes) and provided results of visual analyses to determine if a functional relationship existed between treatment and the dependent variables. The graphic displays are most appropriate for accurate visual inspection. Data reliability (i.e., inter-observer agreements) related to the dependent measures (e.g., reading probes and direct social behavior observations) and treatment fidelity were also reported.
O'Connor, R. E., White, A., & Swanson, H. L. (2007). Repeated reading versus continuous reading: Influences on reading fluency and comprehension. *Exceptional Children, 74,* 31-46.	In a study of two reading interventions (i.e., repeated reading and continuous reading) for increasing reading fluency and comprehension of second- and fourth-grade students, O'Connor, White, and Swanson (2007) reported means, standard deviations, and inferential statistics illustrating outcomes of comparing pretest and posttest scores on various norm-referenced and curriculum-based measures. Additionally, the authors summarized results from a series of mixed model repeated measures analyses to compare the effects of the two interventions. Effect sizes comparing the growth slopes of different conditions (i.e., treatments, control) were also presented in response to the research questions.

Table 5 (Continued)
Examples of Well-Written Results

2. *Well-written results include a summary of all outcomes in relation to research questions and hypotheses.*

Carter, E. W., Trainor, A. A., Sun, Y., & Owens, L. (2009). Assessing the transition-related strengths and needs of adolescents with high-incidence disabilities. *Exceptional Children, 76,* 74-94.	In a study that examined the degree to which educators, parents, and youth converge and diverge in the assessments of 160 high school students' transition-related strengths and needs, Carter, Trainor, Sun, and Owens (2009) reported means, standard deviations, and inferential statistics (e.g., ANOVA, MANOVA) illustrating outcomes related to each of the four research questions. Results were reported in text (with p value and effect sizes), tables, and bar chart format.
Jacobson, L. T., & Reid, R. (2010). Improving the persuasive essay writing of high school students with ADHD. *Exceptional Children, 76,* 157-174.	Jacobson and Reid (2010) reported results in both descriptive and graphic (i.e., single-case design graphic displays) formats on each identified dependent variable to evaluate the effects of a persuasive essay-writing strategy using the self-regulated strategy development model (SRSD) for high school students with attention deficit hyperactivity disorder. The description of the results directly responds to the study hypotheses.

3. *Well-written results include a summary of outcomes as basis for drawing conclusions.*

Lee, S.-H., Wehmeyer, M. L., Soukup, J. H., & Palmer, S. B. (2010). Impact of curriculum modifications on access to the general education curriculum for students with disabilities. *Exceptional Children, 76,* 213-233.	Lee, Wehmeyer, Soukup, and Palmer (2010) reported quantitative results related to each statistical procedure used in the study. Each of the two identified research questions was clearly linked to a specific data analysis procedure and the outcomes were presented respectively based on the data analyses that corresponded to the research questions. Descriptive (e.g., frequencies and percentages) and inferential (e.g., multilevel regression, ANOVA) statistics were reported with acceptable details in both text and tables to support the authors' responses to the research questions.

Santangelo, T. (2009). Collaborative problem solving effectively implemented, but not sustained: A case for aligning the sun, the moon, and the stars. *Exceptional Children*, *75*, 185-209.	Data obtained from observations, interviews, mute evidence (e.g., e-mail correspondence, referral forms, written text materials), and field notes across a 2-year period served as the basis for a qualitative study by Santangelo (2009) to explore the nature and factors associated with successful collaborative problem solving (CPS) implementation within an elementary school. The author organized the results according to the targeted school's CPS implementation status during each year. Key themes observed within each year and critical events occurring between Year 1 and Year 2 that affected the Year 2's CPS implementation were identified and summarized.

Table 6
Examples of Well-Written Discussion

Citation	Explanation
1. *A well-written discussion presents a position, contributes to the development of new knowledge, and/or extends knowledge based on the outcomes of the investigation that was undertaken.*	

Citation	Explanation
Test, D. W., Fowler, C. H., Brewer, D. M., & Wood, W. M. (2005). A content and methodological review of self-advocacy intervention studies. *Exceptional Children, 72,* 101-125.	To address literature limitations, Test, Fowler, Brewer, and Wood (2005) conducted a content and methodological review of interventions designed to promote self-advocacy skills for individuals across disabilities and ages. In discussing the findings of their literature review, the authors identified specific areas for future research in relation to content and methodological implications, respectively. They also suggested several implications for practice to educators in enhancing student self-advocacy.

Citation	Explanation
2. *A well-written discussion ties outcomes to extant literature, compares and contrasts findings with the work of others, and/or extends the perspective of the reader with integrated summaries, guidelines, and implications.*	

Citation	Explanation
McMaster, K., L., Kung, H.-S., Han, I., & Cao, M. (2008). Peer-assisted learning strategies: A "tier 1" approach to promoting English learners' response to intervention. *Exceptional Children, 74,* 194-214.	McMaster, Kung, Han, and Cao (2008) examined the effects of the Kindergarten Peer-Assisted Learning Strategies (K-PALS) with 60 kindergarten English learners (ELs) and non-ELs. The authors discussed their outcomes in relation to existing literature on early reading instruction for ELs, provided research-based recommendations intended to bridge knowledge gap and to strengthen the field's understanding about effective classroom-based beginning reading instruction for ELs, and offered both research and practice implications.

3. *A well-written discussion goes beyond restatement of findings to clarify meaning, pose additional questions, elaborate ideas for future research, and/or articulate the practical value of what was done and discovered.*

Browder, D. M., Ahlgrim-Delzell, L., Courtade, G., Gibbs, S. L., & Flowers, C. (2008). Evaluating the effectiveness of an early literacy program for students with significant developmental disabilities. *Exceptional Children*, 75, 33-52.

Browder, Ahlgrim-Delzell, Courtade, Gibbs, and Flowers (2008) developed Early Literacy Skills Builder (ELSB) curriculum and evaluated the comparative effects of the curriculum versus a traditional sight word approach for 23 participants with significant developmental disabilities. In their "Discussion," the authors went beyond the summary of their findings to interpret the overall meaning of the results, future research questions for investigation, continuing ideas, and practical value inherent in their work. The authors described limitations, pointed to potentials of the developed curriculum for building literature skill of students who are nonverbal or have limited early literacy skills, and discussed implications for future research and improvements in practice.

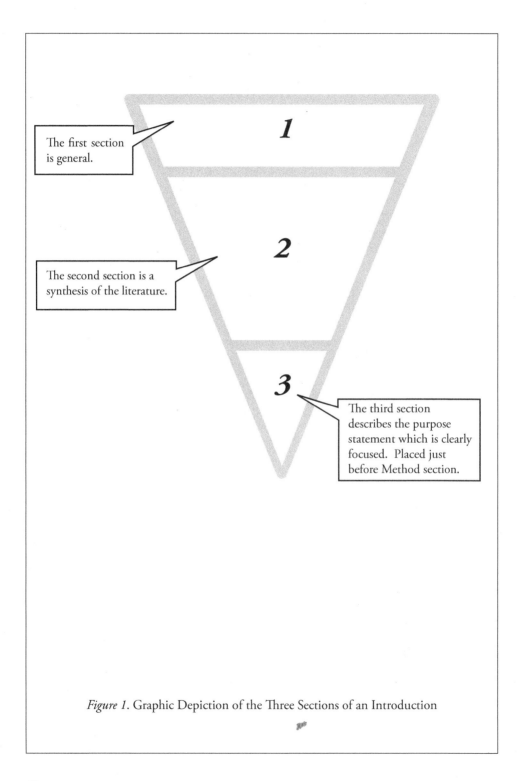

The first section is general.

The second section is a synthesis of the literature.

The third section describes the purpose statement which is clearly focused. Placed just before Method section.

Figure 1. Graphic Depiction of the Three Sections of an Introduction

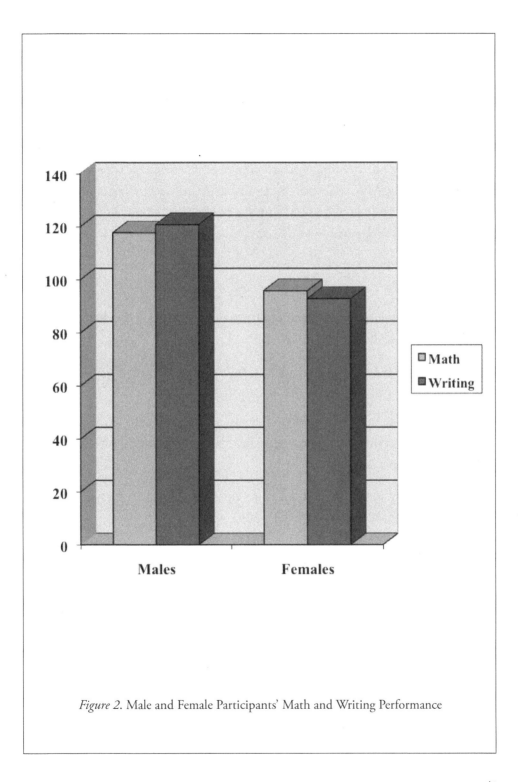

Figure 2. Male and Female Participants' Math and Writing Performance

Appendix A
A Baker's Dozen Style Tips

Style refers to the way in which something is expressed. In writing, it is the way in which a writer conveys meaning or addresses a topic using accepted and appropriate punctuation, spelling, capitalization, and other conventions of print. The following style tips reflect some expected ways to write in research articles guided by APA style (for more information refer to referenced pages and related sections [e.g., Chapter 4] in the *Publication Manual of the American Psychological Association*, 6th ed., 2010).

1. Use brackets to enclose parenthetical material within parentheses (p. 94).

2. Use a single space after punctuation marks in text, reference citations, and initials in names (pp. 87-88).

3. Use data as plural for datum and remember that plural nouns take plural verbs (pp. 78-79).

4. Use Arabic numerals followed by a period to separate paragraphs or sentences (with first word capitalized and last word followed by a period) in a series (pp. 63-65).

5. Use tables to organize and display numerical values or text efficiently in columns and rows (pp. 125-150).

6. Use figures to display information efficiently in graphs, charts, or images other than tables (pp. 150-167).

7. Use direct quotes and reference citations to credit sources for your research (pp. 169-192).

8. Use Times New Roman, with 12-point font size, as preferred typeface (pp. 228-229).

9. Use uniform margins of 1" at top, bottom, and sides of each page (pp. 229).

10. Use double-spacing between all lines of text (p. 229).

11. Use flush-left paragraphs and leave the right margin uneven with a "ragged" edge (p. 229).

12. Use five to seven spaces for indention of paragraphs (p. 229).

13. Use consecutive numbers for each page of the manuscript, beginning with the title page (p. 230).

Source. Adapted from American Psychological Association (APA). (2010). *Publication manual of the American Psychological Association* (6th ed.). Washington, DC: Author.

Appendix B
Review of Key Features of Manuscript Preparation

Begin with a title page that includes a running head, the full title (10 to 12 words) of your manuscript, author names and institutional affiliations, and an author note containing additional information (e.g., funding or other acknowledgments, corresponding author) needed to properly identify and attribute the work. The running head is an abbreviated title that is printed (flush left in all uppercase letters) at the top of each page (APA, 2010, pp. 23-25, 229). Author names and affiliations should reflect contributors and institutions when the research was completed.

An abstract is a brief, comprehensive, and specific summary of your paper (APA, 2010, pp. 25-27, 241). The abstract should start on a new page and be the second page of your manuscript. Type the word Abstract centered on the first line of the page and follow it with between 150 and 250 words describing the content of the manuscript in a left-justified, block-form paragraph. If the manuscript is being prepared using APA style but is not being submitted to a journal for possible publication, an abstract may not be required.

The body of your paper (see APA, 2010, pp. 27-36) will begin on page three, immediately following the abstract. Begin by typing the title of your paper and centering it. The next line should be indented five to seven spaces and begin the introductory section (see APA, 2010, pp. 27-28) of your manuscript focusing on the problem being addressed, why it is important, what is known about it, and what needs to be known (e.g., specific research questions) to extend, expand, and enlighten the knowledge base. After the introduction, include a Method section with subsections detailing the "participants and setting" and the "procedures" describing how the research was completed (see APA, 2010, pp. 29-32). Report the outcomes of your research in the Results section (see APA, 2010, pp. 32-35) and evaluate, interpret, and share implications of them in the Discussion section (see APA, 2010, pp. 35-36).

The reference list follows the body of your text (see APA, 2010, p. 37). It begins on a new page with the word References centered on it. If you only have one reference, type Reference. If your references take up more than one page, *do not* re-type the word References on sequential pages, simply continue your listings with the first line on the next page. Use a "hanging indent" format (i.e., first line is flush left and each subsequent line is indented) for all references. Most word processing programs provide options for setting paragraph styles (e.g., left and right indent set at 0.0 and special or hanging indent set at 0.5 inches).

Footnotes, tables, figures, appendices, and supplementary materials (see APA, 2010, pp. 37-40) follow the reference page(s). Footnotes are used to share additional content. Tables and figures are used to display information in columns and rows or in graphs, charts, or other forms. Appendices are used to share materials and other information that support the study. Supplementary materials include information this is not easily shared with the manuscript, but easily made available in another form (e.g., direct download).

Source. Adapted from American Psychological Association (APA). (2010). *Publication manual of the American Psychological Association* (6th ed.). Washington, DC: Author.

Appendix C
A Few Rules of the Game

When editors refer to style, they usually do not mean writing style; they mean editorial style—the rules a publisher follows to provide clear, consistent dissemination of the printed word (American Psychological Association, APA, 2010, p. 87). The following information summarizes a few generalizations regarding selected functional and technical aspects of APA style.

Abbreviations

Use abbreviations (see APA, 2010, pp. 106-111) sparingly throughout your paper. Always spell out what the abbreviation means the first time it is used and thereafter use the abbreviation. For example, the Behavior and Reading Improvement Center (BRIC) conducted interventions in seven elementary schools; BRIC personnel provided ongoing professional development to administrators, teachers, and other professionals. Abbreviations widely recognized as words (e.g., IQ, AIDS, HIV) may be used without explanation (APA, 2010, p. 107).

Latin Abbreviations

Use English translations of standard Latin terms in nonparenthetical text. Use the following Latin abbreviations in parenthetical material:

cf.	compare	i.e.,	that is,
e.g.,	for example	viz.,	namely,
etc.,	and so forth	vs.	versus, against (APA, 2010, p. 108).

Numbers

Use Arabic numerals with numbers 10 and above (12, 50, and so on) and use words to express numbers 10 and below and use Arabic numerals for all numbers in your abstract and figures (see APA, 2010, pp. 111-114). Note the exception (see APA, pp. 112-113) when combining numerals and words to express back-to-back modifiers in which you use combinations of written and Arabic numerals (e.g., six 2-point scales).. For example, Students in 25 schools participated and all but 5 fourth-grade and 23 eleventh-grade students took the test (*N* = 2345). Spell out the number when beginning a sentence and numbers below 10. To make plurals out of numbers add "s" with no apostrophe (e.g., the 1990s).

Quotation Marks

Use quotation marks to set off the title of an article or chapter in a periodical or book when the title is mentioned in text, to introduce a word or phrase considered slang, an ironic comment, or as an invented or coined expression (see APA, 2010, pp. 91-92). Generally, quotation marks are not needed after the initial use of special terms. For example, the researchers identified age as a "high tolerance" variable, but nothing in the demographic section of the instrument other than age required the high tolerance designation.

Spacing

Use a single space after colons, commas, and semicolons; after periods that separate parts of a reference citation; and, after the periods of the initials in personal names (e.g., R. U. Wright, I. M. Ready); however, do not include a space after internal periods (e.g., A.M., i.e.,) in abbreviations (APA, 2010, pp. 87-88).

Underlining and Italics

Use italics infrequently. Use italics for titles of books, periodicals, films, and videos; introduction of new terms and labels (the first time only); statistical symbols (*t*-test); and, volume titles and volume numbers in reference lists (APA, 2010, pp. 104-106).

Source. Adapted from American Psychological Association (APA). (2010). *Publication manual of the American Psychological Association* (6th ed.). Washington, DC: Author.

Appendix D
Guidelines for the Use of Seriation and Headings

Seriation of syntactically and conceptually similar elements in a series directs the sequence or relationship between them. Headings reflect the organization of the manuscript and establish the importance of each topic. Both of these features promote clarity, conciseness, and comprehension in expository writing (see APA, 2010, pp. 62-65).

Using Seriation

Lengthy or complex elements in sections, paragraphs, or sentences can be made easier to read and follow using seriation. Identify elements in a series by lowercase letters in parentheses or "use commas to separate three or more elements that do not have internal commas" and "use semicolons to separate three or more elements that have internal commas" (APA, 2010, p. 64). Different paragraphs in a series are separated from each other by a number followed by a period. In any series, items are written in parallel form.

Using Headings

When headings are used effectively and appropriately, the organization of the manuscript as well as the content within it is transparent. In the simplest case, a Level 1 heading would be used throughout your paper. Headings are differentiated by numbered levels, from a Level 1 heading to a Level 5. It is not necessary to label headings with numbers or letters (unless instructed to do so for a paper or presentation). The following examples illustrate how each of these levels would be formatted in your manuscript:

Centered, Boldface, Uppercase and Lowercase Heading

Flush Left, Boldface, Uppercase and Lowercase Heading

Indented, boldface, lowercase paragraph heading ending with a period.

Indented, boldface, italicized, lowercase paragraph heading ending with a period.

Indented, italicized, lowercase paragraph heading ending with a period.

Source. Adapted from American Psychological Association (APA). (2010). *Publication manual of the American Psychological Association* (6th ed.). Washington, DC: Author.

Using Headings (Examples)

In general, when using headings follow the conventions for making an outline. For example, if you were writing a literature-based position paper on self-determination, you might divide it using these areas of content: (a) overview of the topic, (b) definitions, (c) interventions, and (d) personal commentary on the topic. Use of a Level 1 heading throughout your paper would be appropriate because each topic is of equal importance; for example:

Self-Determination

Definitions of Self-Determination

Self-Determination Interventions

Perspective on Self-Determination

Townsend (2000) used two levels of headings in examining exclusionary discipline practices and their impact on African American students. Todd, Horner, Newton, Algozzine, Algozzine, and Frank (2010) used three levels of headings in a manuscript about a single-case research study of decision-making practices of school-based teams. The organization of each paper is illustrated in the following examples.

Example 1. Townsend, B. L. (2000). The disproportionate discipline of African American learners: Reducing school suspensions and expulsions. *Exceptional Children, 66,* 381-391.

School Discipline and African American Students

Effects of Exclusionary Discipline on African American Students

School Factors

Cultural Conflicts

Language and Communication

Reducing exclusionary discipline with African American children and youth.

Examining Data

The "So What" Test

Attitudes and Expectations

Classroom Management and Instruction

Cultural Discontinuity

Minimizing Linguistic Barriers

Building Relationships

Participation in School Activities

Increased Interest and Relevance

Family and Community Partnerships

Building Cultural Bridges

Conclusions

Example 2. Todd, A. W., Horner, R. H., Newton, J. S., Algozzine, R. F., Algozzine, K. M., & Frank, J. L. (2010). *Effects of team-initiated problem solving on practices of school-wide behavior support teams*. Manuscript submitted for publication.

Conceptual Foundation

    Problem identification.

    Problem definition.

    Design intervention plan.

    Implement intervention.

    Problem solution.

Training Team-based Problem Solving

Measuring Team-Meeting Practices

Method

Participants and Settings

Measurement

Decision Observation, Recording and Analysis: DORA.

Baseline

Coaching

TIPS Trained

Results

Direct Observation Results

Problem Solving Feedback Form

Discussion

Appendix E
Crediting Sources

Citation of Sources in Text (Example of Level 1 Heading)

The citation of sources is a key element of writing in APA style. *The Publication Manual of the American Psychological Association* (2010) indicates that "whether paraphrasing, quoting an author directly, or describing an idea that influenced your work, you must credit the source" (p. 170). "When quoting, always provide the author, year, and specific page citation . . ." to direct proper attribution (APA, 2010, p. 170). If material is left out within a sentence of the quoted material, indicate it using three spaced ellipsis points (. . .); use four ellipsis points (. . . .) when material is left out between two sentences in quoted material. If inserting explanations in a direct quotation use brackets, not parentheses. If any incorrect spelling, punctuation, or grammar in the source might confuse readers, insert the word *sic*, italicized and bracketed, immediately after the error in the quotation (APA, 2010, p. 172).

Quotations (Example of Level 2 Heading)

 Example 1. (Example of Level 3 Heading). This opinion is shared by many and, of course, ". . . it is easier to raise questions than it is to answer them . . ." (McLeskey, Henry, & Axelrod, 1999, p. 64).

 Example 2. As Townsend (2000) indicates, ". . . school discipline practices disproportionately exclude African American students, especially males, from opportunities to learn" (p. 390).

 With quotations of 40 or more words, *do not* use quotation marks, rather ". . . display [the material] in a freestanding block of text . . ." starting on a new line indented five spaces and indenting each subsequent paragraph as well (APA, 2010, pp. 171).

 Example 3. After a comprehensive study of reading instruction, grouping practices, and outcomes for students with learning disabilities in resource rooms, Moody, Vaughn, Hughes, and Fischer (2000) reached the following conclusions:

Based on the classroom observations and interviews, we do not think that the teachers are solely responsible for the lack of gains these students made. These teachers were providing instruction to too many students to provide the special instruction needed. They carried caseloads that made it extremely difficult to provide students with individualization. Many of the teachers expressed frustration and indicated that they were fed up with what they perceived as impossible teaching, yet they continued to do the best they could for the student's sake. Some teachers were giving up their planning periods and lunches just so they could have smaller groups of students in the resource rooms. Yet they were overwhelmed by their caseloads and frustrated by their inability to give students the time they so desperately needed. (p. 314)

When paraphrasing someone else's material, you are required to cite it. For example, Moody et al. found that special education teachers were frustrated by conditions that they believed were limiting their effectiveness.

References

Make sure that anything referenced in your paper is cited on your Reference page and anything on your Reference page is used in your text. If a paragraph is entirely taken from someone else's thoughts, beliefs, findings, and/or writings, then at the end of the paragraph insert parentheses containing the author's name and year (American Psychological Association, 2010).

All citations in the text contain two parts: The author(s) and year of publication. Always insert the year after the author(s) unless the name of the author is part of the narrative (cf. APA, 2010, pp. 174-192).

Two authors. Always cite both names in text:

According to Skiba and Peterson (2000), school discipline . . . or

. . . based on early intervention research (Sprague & Walker, 2000). or

In 1983, Axelrod and Apsche reported that . . .

Three, four, or five authors. Cite all the authors the first time the reference occurs. In subsequent citations use the first author's surname followed by "et al." and the date (see example below).

Moody, Vaughn, Hughes, and Fischer (2000) found that teachers . . . (first time used). Moody et al. (2000) also found . . . (first subsequent citation per paragraph). Additionally, Moody et al. found . . . (further citations within same paragraph, omit year only if used as part of the narrative).

Six or more authors. In text, cite only the first surname and follow with et al. each time (including the first) the work is cited. For example, Algozzine et al. (1999) studied technology competencies needed by teachers.

Groups as authors. First time cited, spell out the group; for example (American Psychological Association [APA], 2010). Thereafter, in subsequent paragraphs use the abbreviation followed by the publication year. For example, the APA (2010) provides guidance in the preparation of manuscripts for submission to professional journals.

Citation of a work discussed in a secondary source. A primary source is the article, book, or other publication that you have read and used to cite in your paper. In some cases you might wish to use a citation from that work. This is called a secondary source. You should always try to consult the original source. If you cannot, you should cite the source in the text, and refer to the sources you actually read. In the reference section, include only the source that you actually consulted.

For example, suppose you read an article by Townsend (2000) in which she refers to a paper by Riak (1985). If you *did not* actually read Riak (1985) yourself, then in the text, you might say: Riak (as cited in Townsend, 2000) provided a perspective on corporal punishment in school. In the reference section, you would include a reference for Townsend (2000), but *not* for Riak (1985).

Works without identified author(s). "When a work has no identified author, cite in text the first few words of the reference list entry (usually the title) and the year" (APA, 2010, p. 176). For example: As Skiba and Peterson

(2000) noted, "many districts continue to toughen their disciplinary policies" ("Groups Critical," 1999) . . . . When a work's author is "anonymous," cite in text the word Anonymous followed by a comma and the date; for example, (Anonymous, 1997).

Elements and Examples of References in APA Style

The reference section begins on a new page. The references are listed in alphabetical order. Consider authors' names such as McAfee and Macwerner literally; Macwerner would preceed McAfee. For two or more references with the same author, list first whichever one has the earliest publication year, and single author citations precede multiple author citations. If there is no author, the title moves to the author position, and the entry is alphabetized by the first significant word of the title (see APA, 2010, p. 183). When you have two or more references that contain the same author and year, differentiate them by placing a, b, c, d, and so on after the year then use the appropriate year and letter when citing in text. For example:

National Institute of Mental Health. (1994a). *Bipolar disorder* [Brochure]. Indianapolis, IN: Dista Products.

National Institute of Mental Health. (1994b). *Depression* [Brochure]. Indianapolis, IN: Dista Products.

All references should be double-spaced and formatted with a hanging indent and a "paragraph return" at the end of the complete citation (i.e., do not "hit return" at the end of each line in the reference). The following reference formats are examples, and *do not* describe every type of reference. Consult the APA *Publication Manual* for more information (cf. APA, 2010, pp. 193-224).

Required information includes author's surname and initials of first and middle name (if provided), year of publication, title of article, publication information including journal title and volume number in italics followed by inclusive page numbers. Note: If, and only if, each issue of a journal begins on page 1, include the issue number in parentheses immediately after the volume number. "If no publication date is available, write n.d. in parentheses" (APA, 2010, p. 185).

Periodicals With One Author

Algozzine, B. (1980). Single-subject or group research: Is any controversy necessary? *Educational Researcher, 9*(4), 24-25.

Algozzine, B. (1985). Low achiever differentiation: Where's the beef? *Exceptional Children, 52,* 72-75.

Townsend, B. L. (2000). The disproportionate discipline of African American learners: Reducing school suspensions and expulsions. *Exceptional Children, 66,* 381-391.

Periodicals With Multiple Authors

Algozzine, R. F., Antonak, R., Bateman, L. R., Flowers, C. P., Gretes, J. A., Hughes, C. D., & Lambert, R. (1999). Developing technology competencies in a college of education. *Contemporary Education, 70*(4), 26-31.

McLeskey, J., Henry, D., & Axelrod, M. I. (1999). Inclusion of students with learning disabilities: An examination of data from Reports to Congress. *Exceptional Children, 66,* 55-66.

Moody, S. W., Vaughn, S., Hughes, M. T., & Fischer, M. (2000). Reading instruction in the resource room: Set up for failure. *Exceptional Children, 66,* 305-316.

Skiba, R. J., & Peterson, R. L. (2000). School discipline at a crossroads: From zero tolerance to early response. *Exceptional Children, 66,* 335-347.

Spooner, F., Algozzine, B., Thurlow, M., Obiakor, F., & Heller, H. W. (1997). Writing for professional publication: From myth to reality. *Multiple Voices, 2*(1), 12-20.

Sprague, J., & Walker, H. (2000). Early identification and intervention for youth with antisocial and violent behavior. *Exceptional Children, 66,* 367-379.

Unpublished Manuscript With a University Cited

Horner, R. H., Newton, J. S., Todd, A. W., Algozzine, K., & Algozzine, B. (2010). *Using coaches to support problem solving with positive behavior support teams.* Unpublished manuscript, Educational and Community Supports, University of Oregon, Eugene, OR.

Dissertation or Thesis Obtained From Electronic Database

Chambers, A. (2010). *Application of the choicemaker curriculum for teaching self-determination skills to students with emotional and behavioral disabilities in a private day setting.* (Doctoral dissertation). Retrieved from Dissertations & Theses: Full Text. (Publication No. AAT 3389975).

Books

Information needed: Book authors or editors, date of publication, book title, publication information (i.e., location and name of publisher).

James, P. D. (1999). *Time to be in earnest: A fragment of autobiography.* New York, NY: Alfred A. Knopf.

Edited Books

Axelrod, S., & Apsche, J. (Eds.). (1983). *The effects of punishment on human behavior.* New York, NY: Academic Press.

Material in an Edited Book

Duckworth, J. C., & Levitt, E. E. (1994). Minnesota Multiphasic Personality Inventory-2. In D. J. Keyser & R. C. Sweetland (Eds.), *Test critiques: Vol. 10* (pp. 424- 428). Austin, TX: Pro-Ed.

Thurlow, M., Algozzine, B., Edyburn, D. L., & Obiakor, F. E. (2010). Working with editors of research journals. In F. E. Obiakor, B. Algozzine, & F. Spooner (Eds.), *Publish, flourish, and make a difference* (pp. 117-130). Arlington, VA: Council for Exceptional Children.

Groups as Authors

American Psychological Association. (2010). *Publication manual of the American Psychological Association* (6th ed.). Washington, DC: Author.

Note: This is also an example of how to reference editions of books and how to cite when the publisher and author are the same.

Magazine Article

Arie, M. (1996, October 8). Protecting yourself from evil E-mail. *PC Magazine*, *15*(6), 192-193.

Note: Use the exact date for weekly publications. Use the month for monthly publications.

ERIC Document

What Works Clearinghouse. (2007). *Ladders to literacy for kindergarten students. What Works Clearinghouse Intervention Report*. Retrieved from ERIC database. (ED497840)

Personal Communication

Personal communications may be memos, letters, lectures, seminars, interviews, telephone conversations, e-mail, and the like. These types of sources do not provide *recoverable* data and are *not* included in the reference list. Cite personal communications in *text* only. Give the initials as well as the surname of the communicator, and provide as exact a date as possible: W. U. Borst (personal communication, April 7, 1997) said that these are not included in the reference list or (W. U. Borst, personal communication, April 7, 1997)

(See page 179 of the APA *Publication Manual* for more information.)

Sources Retrieved Electronically

Porfeli, E., Wang, C., Audette, R., McColl, A., & Algozzine, B. (2009). Influence of social and community capital on student achievement in a large urban school district. *Education and Urban Society, 42*, 72-95. Retrieved from ERIC database. (Accession No. EJ859995)

Spooner, F., Ahlgrim-Delzell, L., Kohprasert, K., Baker, J., & Courtade, G. (2008). Content analysis of science performance indicators in alternate assessment. *Remedial and Special Education, 29*, 343-351. Retrieved from ERIC database. (Accession No. EJ817620)

For complete guidelines on providing publication information for sources obtained electronically, see pages 187-192 and reference examples (pp. 193-224) in the APA *Publication Manual.*

Works With No Identified Author

Groups critical of no second chances school proposal. (1999, January 27). *The Baltimore Sun*, p. 4B.

Appendix F
Miscellaneous Considerations

Below are a few general things to consider in preparing manuscripts for publication using APA style:

1. Avoid using biased and pejorative language. Do not use "men" to refer to all adults. Some commonly used and acceptable group references include (APA, 2010, pp. 73-77) African Americans, Asian Americans (not Oriental), Latino Americans, Native Americans, sexual orientation (not sexual preference), people with depression and people with AIDS (not depressives or AIDS victims or sufferers), older persons (not elderly), lesbians and gay men (not homosexual). Children who are blind, students with learning disabilities, persons with severe disabilities and other person-first designations are preferred when writing about individuals with disabilities.

2. Avoid presenting more than 27 lines of text per page.

3. Avoid one-sentence paragraphs.

4. Avoid lengthy paragraphs. A paragraph should be no longer than one double-spaced page.

5. Avoid using "popular opinion" publications (i.e., *Time, Newsweek, USA Today, National Enquirer, Redbook*). Use scientific journals for references (i.e., *Exceptional Children, Journal of Educational Psychology, American Educational Research Journal, Behavioral Disorders, Journal of Learning Disabilities, The Journal of Special Education*).

6. Avoid the urge to be creative in preparing your manuscript. Refer to the Grammar and Usage section (see APA, 2010, pp. 77-86) or use the sample papers in the APA *Publication Manual* (cf. APA, 2010, pp. 41-59) as a quick-reference guide.

Most publishers accept authors' word choices unless they convey information that is unclear, inaccurate, or grammatically incorrect. As an organization, APA is "committed both to science and to the fair treatment of individuals and groups, and this policy requires that authors who write for APA publications avoid perpetuating demeaning attitudes and biased assumptions about people in their writing" (APA, 2010, pp. 70-71). The APA *Publication Manual* includes a section addressing guidelines for reducing bias in language (see pp. 70-73); and, the "overall principle for 'nonhandicapping' language is to maintain the integrity (worth) of all individuals as human beings" (APA, 2010, p. 76).

This perspective is clearly in line with the style in special education that includes an emphasis on people-first terminology, the use of terms that support rather than diminish, and language that fosters respect rather than rancor for individuals with disabilities. In practice this means avoiding language that (a) equates people with conditions, (b) has negative connotations, and (c) is regarded as derogatory, disrespectful, or degrading. It also means that terms like "general education students" and "special education students" are less preferred than "students with disabilities" and "students without disabilities," because the former might imply a distinction of inferiority (as if "general" is good and "special" is bad) or separation (as in "them" *vs.* "us"), whereas the latter does not (i.e., it more reflects a statement of fact, as in "students in the experimental group" and "students in the control group"). Additionally, the term "students with disabilities" is preferred as opposed to terms like "general education students" and "special education students" because a significant proportion of students with disabilities now receive their education in general education classrooms.

Source. Adapted from American Psychological Association (APA). (2010). *Publication manual of the American Psychological Association* (6th ed.). Washington, DC: Author.

Appendix G
Reviews, Reviewers, Reviewing, and Electronic Manuscript Submission and Review Systems

An important value of publishing is to extend and disseminate knowledge about our world. Professors engage in professional writing activities (e.g., publishing articles, reviewing manuscripts, engaging in editorial service) to enhance their teaching, to provide service to their profession, and to advance their careers by contributing to tenure and promotion expectations for research, scholarship, and service. Administrators and teachers write to extend the knowledge base and improve educational practice. Students write as a part of professional indoctrination practices that many believe is essential in quality undergraduate and graduate programs. Few of these authors have escaped the professional writing experience and review process without rejection. In fact, many authors who have been successful have learned to turn negative responses into resubmissions and further improvement. Unfortunately, few (especially those new to the professorate or technical writing) have received any formal preparation in the rites of passage and practice associated with responding to reviews, working with reviewers, or serving as a reviewer for the work of others; and most are unprepared to do so competently (cf. Golde & Dore, 2001). In response to these needs, some professional organizations have begun to offer workshops, panel sessions, or editors' sessions at conferences to offer tips or guidelines to early career faculty or graduate students who are new to publishing or reviewing. For instance, the Division for Research (DR) of the Council for Exceptional Children (CEC) has offered an Early Career Research Workshop at the CEC Annual Convention since 2006 for tenure accruing faculty in special education in the first 3 to 4 years of their career to learn from seasoned colleagues strategies for navigating the early years of their higher education career. An important topic for the workshop is "Writing for Publication." Similarly, the annual International Conference on Learning Disabilities of the Council for Learning Disabilities (CLD) also schedules a "Meet the Editors" session for journal editors in the area of learning disabilities to discuss the scope of the selected journals, manuscript submission guidelines, and the respective review process. Some discussions or presentations about publishing at a conference result in a published article for wide dissemination (e.g., Klingner, Scanlon, & Pressley, 2005). In supporting the aforementioned efforts in preparing effective authors and reviewers, we offer some advice on reviews, reviewers, and reviewing in the sections that follow. Additionally, due to the advancement in technology and the popularity of electronic review process usage for many professional journals, we briefly describe the electronic manuscript submission and peer review systems.

Reviews

To be successful in publishing, one must be willing to turn obstacles into opportunities and this means making the most of editorial reviews. Henson (1995), in a review of writing for publication, suggested that the acceptance rate on the average for journals in education (e.g., *Action in Teacher Education, Educational Leadership, Phi Delta Kappan, Review of Educational Research*) is about 33%. Based on their experiences as journal editors and authors, Klingner et al. (2005) indicated that the acceptance rate for some highly regarded journals in education is often one in five (i.e., 20%). Similarly, low rates of acceptance are common in special education. For example, in a report to the readership of the *Exceptional Children* journal, Graham (2009) reported the acceptance rate for volume 75 (Fall 2008 – Summer 2009) as approximately 20%. According to the 2010 Publisher's annual report for *The Journal of Special Education* (Sage Publications, 2010), the acceptance rate for the year of 2009 for the journal is approximately 25%. This means that about two thirds to three quarters of the time, a manuscript will not be accepted if no resubmission to another journal takes place.

When a manuscript is submitted to a refereed journal for consideration for publication, it will undergo a peer-review process in which members of the journal's editorial review board or selected guest reviewers with expertise in the content of the manuscript will be asked to thoroughly critique the manuscript. A review process is "refereed" when a journal employs a peer-review process to involve reviewers in making a judgment on the quality and suitability of a manuscript for publication. Typically, manuscript reviewers write a set of narrative comments about the paper, respond to a checklist rating the manuscript's acceptability for the journal which includes strengths and weaknesses, and make a recommendation about publishing the paper (e.g., accept as is, accept with revisions, reject-revise-resubmit, or reject). The purpose of the peer-review process is to ensure quality of papers that will be made available to the public. The recommendations of the reviewers are then transmitted to the editor, who then uses those reviews to formulate an editorial decision that is then communicated to the author(s).

Our collective experience suggests that very little goes through the review process unscathed; in most instances, the author will be responding to recommendations to revise the manuscript. At a very basic level, the process of responding to recommendations for revision is learning to deal with rejection, or learning to turn "lemons into lemonade."

Typical outcomes and recommendations for a manuscript submitted to a journal usually fall into one of four groups: (a) accept as is; (b) accept with revisions; (c) reject, revise, and resubmit; and (d) reject. We discuss each decision in the following sections.

Accept As Is

This outcome, *accept as is*, is usually a very low probability (Baker, 2002; Klingner et al., 2005). Based on the process and intent of a manuscript submitted for potential inclusion in a respected professional journal, the editors and the reviewers usually recommend some type of change. Changes at this level could involve basic style editing, including adherence to the style specifications (e.g., reference list) of the American Psychological Association (APA, 2010), or adding or deleting sections to more closely comply with the style, tone, and purpose of the journal. This is not to say that manuscripts are never accepted without changes. Recommendations for change more reflects the reality that even an "acceptable" paper can be fine-tuned and improved in the publication process.

Accept With Revisions

If a research manuscript is appropriate for the journal to which it is submitted, the content is articulated clearly, and the methodology is appropriate and well-documented, *accept with revisions* is a common outcome. The degree to which revisions are recommended may be minor (e.g., adding new citations, shortening length of the manuscript, adding/deleting tables or figures) or substantial (e.g., rewriting or reorganizing paper, adding new subsections or information). In either case, it is important to take a moment to celebrate (that the work is not rejected!) and immediately move on to carefully address the reviewers' and editor's recommendations for a timely resubmission. Timely and successful revisions which meet with the editor's satisfaction, accompanied by a cover letter detailing how you addressed the suggestions, are key to final acceptance. However, at times, the editor or a reviewer may have clearly misunderstood a point that was being made in the manuscript. In these cases, politely and succinctly address the issue and explain or justify in the cover letter why a revision for that certain suggestion is not appropriate.

Responding to editor's and reviewers' comments is, in most cases, a necessary part of professional writing. Receiving requests for revisions is an expected positive outcome of the editorial process. Following are some recommendations in responding to editor's and reviewers' comments.

- Think positively; "anything but a rejection is an encouraging sign" and reviewers' comments are intended to improve the quality of your work (Holschuh, 1998, p. 6).

- Find ways to keep the manuscript "alive" within the requested deadline.

- Do the suggested modifications as part of your regular writing schedule.

- Carefully respond to reviewers' and editor's suggestions unless doing so conflicts with the original purpose of the work, in which case, justify your reasons.

- Contact the editor if there are any unclear comments or if you cannot meet the suggested deadline.

- Keep track of the changes you have made to the manuscript and include them in a cover letter indicating what changes were made and where (e.g., page number), and/or rationales for why certain changes were not made.

- Send the revised manuscript to another journal if the resubmission is not accepted.

Reject, Revise, and Resubmit

Some special education journals such as *The Journal of Special Education* or *Teacher Education and Special Education* have a specific editorial decision called *reject, revise, and resubmit*. Other journals like *Research and Practice for Persons with Severe Disabilities* (*RPSD*) have a category labeled "do not publish/invite revision," that communicates a similar meaning to the author. A manuscript that receives this category of decision may indicate that it has some potential contribution to the field but presents one or more critical flaws in the theoretical framework, methodology, data analyses, and/or conclusions, therefore warranting a rejection in its current form. Unlike a manuscript accepted with major revisions, a decision of "reject, revise, and resubmit" typically signifies that the revised and resubmitted work will undergo a new review process, with a new manuscript number and different reviewers.

Despite the disappointment of receiving such an editorial decision, it is most helpful to carefully consider the reviewers' and editor's comments and use the "invited" opportunity to substantially improve the quality of your work. Again, the "invitation" for a resubmission is a positive deliberation that indicates a potential value and confirms the importance of your work to the journal. Positive thinking and determination to move on to revision and resubmission is more likely to take you to a successful acceptance. In fact, Henson (1995) points out that if an editor makes a recommendation that a manuscript be revised, 75% of those revised manuscripts go on to be published.

For any author, suggested revisions provide an opportunity to establish a writing schedule. With some journals, the editor will specify a deadline by which he or she would like to receive the revised manuscript. With other journals, the deadline for revision is left open-ended. In either case, it is important not to delay the revision (as it will increase the likelihood that the manuscript will sit on your desk for months) and meet the editor's schedule, or communicate challenges to the editor if there are some major obstacles that prohibit revising the manuscript in a timely fashion. Usually, the recommendations for changes at this level are lengthy and it is possible that some of the changes could be in conflict with one another based on the position taken by the reviewers. It will be important to thoroughly consider each recommendation in your revision, but provide a justification in the cover letter to the editor if you choose not to make certain changes. On rare occasions, authors may opt to submit the revised manuscript elsewhere without resubmitting to the same journal if they perceive the majority of the required revisions to be in conflict with their views or research purposes. In this case, it is simply a courtesy to inform the editor about your decision to not resubmit your work to the journal.

Reject

An editorial decision suggesting that the manuscript has been *rejected* can come in two major forms. First, the rejection happens "out-of-hand" by the editor, with the manuscript never sent out for review. This decision is possibly due to one or more of several possible reasons: (a) content inappropriate for the journal or falling outside the scope/mission of the journal, (b) lack of adherence to the manuscript submission guidelines (e.g., page length recommendations significantly violated, extensive APA infractions or stylistic errors), or (c) overall presentation of the manuscript is of insufficient quality to be sent out for peer reviews (e.g., Holschuh, 1998; Klingner et al., 2005). Following are several ways to avoid or overcome this form of rejection.

- Carefully attend to the author guidelines specified in the editorial policy for the journal to which you are submitting. Adherence to the manuscript submission guidelines can create a good first impression of your manuscript.

- Submit your manuscript only when you are sure that you have done your best work. Although peer reviewers are one of the most constructive, objective feedback forms you may receive for your writing, they are not intended for "proofreading." Manuscripts with careless writing or stylistic errors can often irritate reviewers and the editor, therefore greatly decreasing the odds of it being reviewed positively, or the worst, of being sent out for reviews.

- Solicit support from colleagues or mentors to objectively review your manuscript and to provide feedback before your submission to a journal. Seasoned colleagues can often provide useful input regarding the match between your manuscript and the journal as well as the overall quality of your manuscript.

The second type of rejection occurs when the editor has received reviewers' recommendations and feels that the manuscript presents problematic issues that are too great to be revised in meeting the criteria acceptable for publication in the journal. In their annual report to the readership of *Exceptional Children*, Algozzine and Thurlow (2000) listed the following as "typical problems" that were identified in manuscripts rejected by field reviewers, associate editors, and editors: (a) insufficient need identified in literature review or introduction, (b) unclear statement of purpose for the research, (c) inadequate sample or insufficient description of participants to warrant generalization, (d) insufficient description of technical adequacy of dependent data, (e) inadequate presentation of results, (f) insufficient outcomes to warrant dissemination, and (g) overgeneralization relative to scope of study. In her role as a past associate editor of the *Teaching and Teacher Education* (*TATE*), Alton-Lee (1998) collated reviewers' criticisms from 142 reviews of 58 manuscripts submitted to *TATE* from April 1997 to April 1998. She described 13 categories most frequently identified by reviewers as areas of criticisms that affected the quality of submitted manuscripts. The top six most recurring areas of criticisms included: (a) lack of methodological transparency, adequacy, and rationale; (b) unsupported or unjustified claims or conclusions; (c) weakness in formats (e.g., poor writing style, inconsistent formatting, lack of coherence between sections); (d) unclear rationale for the theoretical framework; (e) inadequate and inconsistent data analyses; and (f) inadequacies in literature review. Similarly, Baker (2002) identified the two most serious flaws in manuscripts that lead to a decision of rejection, including (a) the research lacks a guiding or well-grounded theoretical framework, and (b) the problem or question of interest is of no importance to the field or is outdated. Although particularly specific to the *Journal of Workplace Learning*, Kekale, de Weerd-Nederhof, Cervai, and Borelli (2009) also identified similar problems in submitted manuscripts that often led to rejection. These identified problems included (a) expanding conclusions beyond the reported data, (b) not reporting findings in understandable language/terms, (c) failing to provide a strong rationale for the identified research, and (d) failing to establish conclusions in relation to the research questions or hypotheses.

Regardless of the reasons for rejection, authors can easily come away disappointed, but typically are also given constructive information that can be used in revising and submitting the manuscript to another journal or in developing more rigorous research in the future. As difficult as it is, one of the best things to do is to thoroughly examine the critique, including each of the reviews and the letter from the editor, to see what can be learned from the comments. To paraphrase Richard Nixon in a note written in July 1969, in reference to Edward Kennedy and the Chappaquiddick Bridge incident: *Defeat doesn't finish a person--quitting does. A person is not finished when defeated. A person is finished when he or she quits* (as cited in Safire, 1975). Here is a rule from successful writers: *Do not quit!* Although the reviews can be overwhelming initially, any further review of the decision letter and reviewers' comments can become more manageable, useful, and clearer. It is often helpful to get another opinion from a respected faculty member who will not just side with you, but give you an honest professional judgment. If the current effort is truly insufficient for publication, then use the feedback from the rejected paper to avoid making the same mistakes again on the next research study and write-up. Successful and productive professional writers turn obstacles into opportunities. Often, this means making the most of less-than-perfect editorial reviews, or put simply, dealing positively with rejection.

Reviewers

As indicated previously, the "refereed" review process ensures the quality of the accepted manuscripts for publication. Refereed journals rely on a cadre of content experts to judge the appropriateness of manuscripts submitted for publication. Articles published in refereed journals are sometimes weighted more heavily in professional development deliberations (e.g., tenure and promotion reviews) because these publications represent acceptance by a panel of peers considered experts. Typically, reviewers do not know the identity of the author(s) of the manuscript they are reviewing and the identity of the reviewers is not shared with the author(s). This is known as "double blind review."

Often, the journal editors develop a list of reviewer guidelines for reviewers to follow when evaluating a manuscript and constructing a review as a way to foster objectivity in the review. For authors, knowing what reviewers are looking for in manuscripts under review is a good place to start when writing for publications. Understanding the expectations for acceptance can likely support writers in achieving better quality in their work.

Reviewer Guidelines

Although reviewer guidelines may vary widely across journals, and editors and reviewers scrutinize many aspects of a manuscript, perhaps no two features are more important than *the overall quality of the research under investigation* and *the presentation of the study itself* (Uchiyama & Simone, 1999). Specifically, most criteria for evaluating a manuscript involve a reviewer's assessment on each of the major sections of a manuscript (i.e., Introduction, Method, Results, and Discussion) to determine its quality, acceptability, and appropriateness for the journal. For example, Baker (2002) listed several questions that reviewers may use as a guide to review a manuscript (pp. 175-176):

- Is the literature review current, does it situate the study in a body of research, is it related to the research question or problem, and does it present a guiding theoretical framework?

- Does the methodology adequately describe the setting or intervention, the participants, the data gathering instruments or techniques, and the data analysis? Does it provide a rationale for the design of the study and is the design appropriate for the research problem?

- Do the results address the research problem or question and are they presented in a way that adds to the understanding of the study?

- Are the conclusions supported by the data in a convincing manner? Are the conclusions used to explore the implications of the study . . . of importance to the [field]?

To help authors prepare a manuscript for review and publication before submission, Uchiyama and Simone (1999) also provided a series of questions authors may use to guide their work (see Table G-1). Additional questions and guidelines categorized by the four major sections of a manuscript are also available in Table G-2. Although these questions and tips are not definitive, they can be useful to authors in preparing an acceptable manuscript by helping them understand what aspects reviewers are expecting to see in a manuscript.

Expectations for Reviewers

Fields such as special education depend on individuals willing to serve as reviewers. Reviewers are typically professionals with expertise in content areas as well as in the process of reviewing. Serving as a reviewer is a professional practice to be taken seriously. Expectations for their behavior help establish the integrity of the process and instill confidence in it. First, if a reviewer feels that he or she is unqualified or lacks the time to fairly judge the manuscript assigned, the reviewer is expected to return the manuscript promptly to the editor so as not to compromise or delay the review process. Second, when a manuscript is submitted to a journal following APA guidelines, reviewers "may not, without authors' explicit permission, quote from a manuscript under review or circulate copies of it for any purpose other than editorial review" (APA, 2010, p. 19). Further, if a reviewer consults with a colleague about a manuscript, the editor should be informed. Third, reviewers are expected to objectively judge the quality of a manuscript on its represented merit; personal criticism or unprofessional responses are never appropriate. If a manuscript submitted for review presents a potential conflict of interest or the reviewer has a biased opinion with regard to it, the reviewer is expected to return the manuscript promptly without review and to advise the editor. If a reviewer suspects or knows that a manuscript is authored or co-authored by a person with whom the reviewer has a personal or professional relationship, the information should be brought to the attention of the editor. Finally, professional wisdom also dictates that matters of style are expected in professional writing and reviewers are expected to verify adherence to them. As a result, it is important for a reviewer to check and double check the written review carefully for typographical errors, just like an author would for the manuscript or an editor for the decision letter.

Reviewing

Accepted reviewing practices in special education follow guidelines set forth by the American Psychological Association. In this regard,

> [r]eviewers provide the editor with evaluations of a manuscript on the basis of their assessment of the scholarly quality of the manuscript, the importance of the novel contribution that the work might provide, and the appropriateness of the work to the particular journal. The decision to accept a manuscript, to reject it, or to invite a revision is the responsibility of the editor; the editor's decision may differ from the recommendation of any or all of the reviewers. (APA, 2010, pp. 226-227)

Clearly, editors depend on reviewers to establish and maintain the quality of their journals and to foster and sustain the integrity of the review process. Serving as a reviewer (i.e., reviewing) requires time, expertise, and commitment; with the typical competing priorities facing special education professionals, the question "Why Review?" deserves consideration.

Baker (2002) identified reviewing as "a self-regulating mechanism that shapes a field" (p. 179). Reviewers' and editors' feedback and recommendations can often contribute to the refinement of focus or scope of manuscripts being published in journals. For example, since the publication of the 2005 special issue of *Exceptional Children* addressing the "Criteria for Evidence Based Practice in Special Education ("Criteria," 2005) attention to using the identified quality indicators for evaluating studies with various types of research methodologies has become more common. The greater rigor and sophistication in research quality partly demands higher expectations from the authors and reviewers; the reviewers' and editors' expectations shape the quality of submitted manuscripts. Reviewing also provides opportunities to participate in the enhancement of knowledge as well as to take advantage of the dissemination of knowledge. In fact, reviewers typically see "cutting edge" research months before it is published; by reviewing manuscripts, reviewers have opportunities to help authors improve the effectiveness of their message and to strengthen the presentation of it. Additionally, reviewing offers opportunities to improve one's own writing by critically evaluating the work of others. Reviewing is also a positive way to network with other professionals and the experience can lead to letters of support from editors at key professional development crossroads. Further, reviewing is one way to both contribute to and take advantage of the peer-review process that prevails in promoting scholarship in one's own profession.

Blake Ives, Senior Editor for *Management Information System Quarterly* in 1992, provides a well-crafted statement reflecting what a well-written review adds to the publication process. His comments, approaching reviewing from a Total Quality Management perspective, have relevance to reviewing in special education.

> A high quality reviewer can add value in many ways. She can highlight the strengths as well as the weaknesses of the article. She can provide useful references (with citations). She can provide new analysis opportunities, alternative theoretical underpinnings, different explanations for results, communications improvements, a clearer focus, further extensions, implications for practice, and even suggestions for rewriting that can reposition the work so as to avoid the fatal errors. A reviewer can also add value by informing the editor of the areas of the review that he feels qualified (or unqualified) to comment on. For instance, if you are unfamiliar with the particular statistical technique or some of the literature, let the editor know. The good reviewer is also sensitive to the author's feelings and, even while rejecting a submission, might offer encouragement, suggest alternative outlets, or propose new modes of attack. On the other hand, most editors find sarcastic or demeaning reviews to be unprofessional, unjustifiable, and disagreeable. A reviewer must never forget that an author's career may be riding on this article or even this review. In other instances, you will be looking at a new graduate's first publication attempt. (Ives, 1992, para. 10)

Despite the benefits of reviewing for publications, most writing manuals provide little or no information about reviewing or writing an effective review. To help fill this gap, we rely on some fundamental principles that are distilled from years of reading and writing editorial reviews. Above all, a good review encourages and elevates more than it discourages and denigrates. Following are some guidelines or tips for conducting an effective review.

- Assume that you share a common perspective or point of view with the author. A concept underlying this process is judgment of and by peers. No one prepares a manuscript for publication that he or she believes is unworthy of review. Share the enthusiasm of the author that the work that has been done was necessary and important. Look for and acknowledge positive aspects of the work and only reluctantly see or report otherwise.

- Write to convince, not convert, the author. Again, the author has presented the best case. If inadequacies are evident, they should be clearly identified (and, if possible, countered with alternative arguments). Document the basis for any decision that is made (including "accept as is"). When writing a review, ask yourself if it would be considered evenhanded and helpful if you received it in response to a manuscript you submitted to a professional journal.

- Do not convert editors and authors into detectives. Clearly pinpoint specific areas that are the source of any strengths or weaknesses in a study and that contribute to any decision regarding it. If important information is missing, let the editor and author know about it.

- Do not assume that authors know everything. Avoid absolute positions on issues that are open to question. Assume, at least on first reading, that authors have adequate knowledge regarding the topic under investigation and use conditional, rather than condescending language in your review. Consider feedback such as "Perhaps I missed something, but evidence for the technical adequacy of the observation system was limited" over "No data were provided on technical adequacy, therefore, the observation system has no value."

- Do not hold authors to impossible standards. When you think an author did not use the best design or analysis, point out alternatives; however, avoid being overly critical. Sometimes the best is not possible given constraints and exigencies evident in "field" research, and approximations, although limited, still add to the knowledge base. Further, keep in mind that sometimes "ideals" are a matter of opinion. Expect justification and request it or provide alternative perspectives that are informative.

- Write reviews that encourage authors. Focus on aspects in the manuscript that you are most competent to judge. Your expertise will carry with it respect for your opinions and help authors to take them seriously. Use economy, clarity, and conviction in your writing. Just as you attempt to understand the manuscript, the editor and author will attempt to understand your review; provide as much assistance as you can. Illustrate the good with the bad and "don't miss the forest for the trees." Often, the big picture (e.g., Is the conceptual framework clear? Does the field need another study demonstrating that reinforcement works? Are the conclusions appropriate and grounded in the study?) is overlooked in the search for problems (e.g., sample size, analysis) that characterize the approach taken by some reviewers.

- Assume that your review is expected to add to the publication process. Check the adequacy and accuracies of citations; suggest additions as appropriate. Pay attention to style and point out problems that detract from the presentation. When you have an overly negative reaction to a manuscript, confirm the inappropriate aspects of it with a colleague. Supply recommendations for improving the work.

Because all authors dislike long review times, be prompt in returning your review and analysis. If you are unable to complete the review by the designated deadline when being asked, inform the editor immediately so that reassignment of the manuscript to another reviewer is possible.

Furthermore, in *Time to Be in Earnest*, novelist P. D. James (1999) discusses "a list of somewhat presumptuous advice for reviewers" (p. 93).

Modified and augmented slightly here, these recommendations offer some additional guidance when thinking about reviewing.

1. Always read the whole article before you write your review.

2. Don't undertake to review an article if it is written on a topic you particularly dislike.

3. Review the article the author wrote, not the one you think should have been written.

4. If you have prejudices—and you are entitled to them—face them frankly and, if appropriate, acknowledge them.

5. Avoid being deliberately or inadvertently cruel.

6. If you absolutely hate the article and have nothing interesting, constructive, or positive to say about it, why review it?

7. If you are given an article to review by a close friend and you strongly dislike it, don't review it (none of us like hurting our friends and the temptation to be overly kind is too strong).

8. Resist the possibility of using a review to pay back old scores or vent your dislikes, hostilities, or negative opinions.

9. Read what you have written and ask yourself if you would be pleased to receive it as a review of your work (if not, rewrite it).

In supporting James's (1999) recommendations, Zmud's (1998) direct set of desirable reviewing behaviors supplements the field's expectations for effective reviewers.

1. Agree to review manuscripts when asked, but only when they address areas in your expertise.

2. Return the review as quickly as you can; get it off your desk.

3. Do not agree to perform a review if you cannot turn it around quickly.

4. Read the manuscript twice before beginning the review.

5. Identify strengths, weaknesses, and fatal flaws before writing your review.

6. Identify ideas or information that might add materially to a manuscript's value.

7. Identify how weaknesses can be resolved and provide suggestions for resolving them.

8. Provide suggestions or directions for improving on a manuscript's strengths.

9. Present your assessment and recommendations in a positive style and tone.

Ultimately, the best advice in preparing a review is to present an analysis that you would be pleased to receive were the work your own.

Electronic Manuscript Submission and Review System

Over the past decade, there has been an increase in electronic review process usage to replace the traditional postal mail, hard-copy paper peer-review process for many professional journals. The proliferation of electronic review adoption is intended to simplify the manuscript submission and review process, streamline administrative tasks related to process manuscripts, increase cost-effectiveness of the peer review process (e.g., eliminating mailing and paper distribution costs, reducing time to assign reviewers and make an editorial decision), and provide a more effective and efficient way to store or track all of the submitted manuscripts across years. Although the adoption of electronic manuscript submission and review systems (e.g., Editorial Manager™, own system unique to the journal) varies from journal to journal, many education journals and publishers use ScholarOne Manuscripts™ (formerly known as Manuscript Central) for their online manuscript submission and peer-review process. According to the ScholarOne Fact Sheet (Thomson Reuters, 2009), it serves more than 365 societies and publishers, over 3,400 books and journals, and 13 million registered users. For example, 21 journals in special education (e.g., *Career Development for Exceptional Individuals, Focus on Autism and Other Developmental Disabilities, Intervention in School and Clinic, Journal of*

Disability Policy Studies, Journal of Emotional and Behavioral Disorders, Journal of Positive Behavior Interventions, Teacher Education and Special Education, The Journal of Special Education) produced by the Sage Publications use ScholarOne Manuscripts™.

Regardless of which electronic manuscript submission and peer-review systems are used, such a system typically has built-in functions and infrastructures that are unique to editors, reviewers, and authors, respectively, based on their roles and needs. Accessibility to these specific functions is available upon log-in with own user ID and password. For example, in ScholarOne Manuscripts™, editors and administrative officers (e.g., journal production editor) typically have access to the Editorial Office Center, Production Center, and EIC (Editor in Chief) Center, in addition to the Author Center and the Reviewer Center. The Editorial Office Center allows editors (including managing editor) to (a) screen submitted manuscripts for appropriateness and complete an administrative checklist to reject a manuscript without sending out for reviews or process it for reviewer selection and assignment; (b) access, download, and upload author manuscript files in their original forms (Word, Excel, or image files); (c) track all electronic correspondences (e.g., e-mails) and actions taken (e.g., assigning reviewers, updating information); (d) access and edit reviewer comments; (e) construct onscreen decision letters using editable letter templates; (f) program and receive automated e-mail notices for assignments and overdue tasks; and (g) perform multiple statistics reports regarding the journal (e.g., acceptance rate, turn-around time, number of manuscripts receiving certain decisions), among other functionalities. The Author Center enables an author to submit new manuscripts by following a list of steps for inputting information and uploading manuscript files. An author can track their current and past manuscripts regarding the manuscript status (e.g., awaiting administrative checklist, awaiting reviewer assignment, awaiting reviewer scores, awaiting EIC decision), and contact the editorial office for any inquiries about a submitted manuscript. The Reviewer Center is only available to reviewers who have access to the assigned manuscripts (in HTML or PDF documents) and contains the score sheet on which the reviewers are to make a recommendation (e.g., Accept, Minor Revision, Major Revision, Reject) and to submit their review supporting their recommendation. Additionally, The Reviewer Center lists all of the past manuscripts a reviewer has processed with posted comments, recommendations for decision, and the editor's final editorial decision.

With the convenience and accessibility of electronic manuscript submission and peer-review systems, authors, reviewers, and editors are now able to experience a more effective and efficient way to submit and track manuscripts, access and provide reviews, and process and make decisions about manuscripts in a more timely manner. Whether a journal is adopting an electronic manuscript submission and peer-review system, it is always best to familiarize yourself with the editorial policy of the journal to which you are submitting your manuscript to ensure a smooth manuscript submission process.

Appendix G References

Algozzine, B., & Thurlow, M. (2000). Annual report to the readership from the editors of *Exceptional Children. Exceptional Children, 66,* 571-572.

Alton-Lee, A. (1998). A troubleshooter's checklist for prospective authors derived from reviewers' critical feedback. *Teaching and Teacher Education, 14,* 887-890.

American Psychological Association. (2010). *Publication manual of the American Psychological Association* (6th ed.). Washington, DC: Author.

Baker, D. (2002). The peer review process in science education journals. *Research in Science Education, 32,* 171-180.

Criteria for evidence-based practice in special education. (2005). [Special Issue]. *Exceptional Children, 71*(2).

Golde, C. M., & Dore, T. M. (2001). *At cross purposes: What the experiences of today's doctoral students reveal about doctoral education.* Madison, WI: University of Wisconsin, Wisconsin Center for Education Research. Retrieved from www.phd-survey.org

Graham, S. (2009). Report to the readership. *Exceptional Children, 76,* 126-127.

Henson, K. T. (1995). *The art of writing for publication.* Boston, MA: Allyn and Bacon.

Holschuh, J. L. (1998). Editorial: Why manuscripts get rejected and what can be done about it: Understanding the editorial process from an insider's perspective. *Journal of Literacy Research, 30,* 1-7. doi:10.1080/10862969809547979

Ives, B. (1992). Editor's comments. *Management Information Systems Quarterly, 16*(2). Retrieved from http://www.misq.org/archivist/vol/no16/issue2/edstat.html

James, P. D. (1999). *Time to be in earnest.* New York, NY: Alfred A. Knopf.

Kekale, T., de Weerd-Nederhof, P., Cervai, S., & Borelli, M. (2009). The "dos and don'ts" of writing a journal article. *Journal of Workplace Learning, 21,* 71-80. doi:10.1108/13665620910924925

Klingner, J. K., Scanlon, D., & Pressley, M. (2005). How to publish in scholarly journals. *Educational Researcher, 34,* 14-20. doi:10.3102/0013189X034008014

Safire, W. (1975). *Before the fall: An inside view of the pre-Watergate White House.* Garden City, NY: Doubleday.

Sage Publications. (2010). *The Journal of Special Education: Annual report 2010.* Thousand Oaks, CA: Author.

Thomson Reuters. (2009). *ScholarOne Manuscripts™: The online manuscript submission and peer review process.* Retrieved from http://scholarone.com/media/manuscripts_fs.pdf

Uchiyama, K., & Simone, G. (1999). *Publishing educational research: Guidelines and tips.* Washington, DC: American Educational Research Association. Retrieved from http://www.aera.net/uploadedFiles/Journals_and_Publications/Journals/pubtip.pdf

Zmud, B. (1998). Editor's comments. *Management Information Systems Quarterly*, *22*(3). Retrieved from http://misq.org/archivist/vol/no22/issue3/edstat.html#state

Table G-1
Criteria for Judging Manuscripts: Questions to Ask About Research and Presentation

Topic	Questions
Design	• Have the parameters for the research questions and overall design been clearly established? • Is the central issue or problem of your research stated effectively? • Have you situated your research and ideas within pertinent literature, showing how your work builds upon the work of others? • Does your research push the boundaries of current research, and make (in your estimation) a significant contribution to the literature? • Is the data collection and analysis systematic and appropriate?
Conceptual Framework	• Have you carefully designed and articulated the framework of your study? • Have you included, where appropriate, relevant sources on the topic (not necessarily listing everything that has been written by everyone)?
Coherence	• Is the main argument or premise clearly stated and logical? Is the text organized to clarify your argument or premise? In other words, can readers follow your thinking throughout the piece?
Content	• Is the content connected within and among sections of your paper? • Does the abstract provide an overall representation of your manuscript?
Clarity of Information	• Have you presented information (tables, graphs, general analyses) with your audience in mind? Be sure to check assumptions about readership being familiar (or not) with local issues, policies, or technical language.
Clarity of Data	• Have you presented data in an understandable layout and explained findings to clearly support your argument?

Format	• Does the format of your manuscript conform to the style guidelines used by the journal?
	• Have you avoided biased language? Used current terminology (e.g., participants rather than subjects)? Explained abbreviations or acronyms? Demystified jargon? Avoided the overuse of metaphors? Used correct mechanics (grammar, punctuation)?

Note. Adapted from *Publishing educational research: Guidelines and tips*, by K. Uchiyama and G. Simone, 1999, Washington, DC: American Educational Research Association.

Table G-2
Questions and Guidelines for Authors to Prepare a Manuscript Before Submission

Section	Questions	Guidelines/Tips
Introduction	• Why is your research needed? • What are two or three key points the reader needs to know before reading what you did? • Is your tone positive?	• Provide a clear indication of a significant and important problem. • Provide adequate, relevant, and appropriate background for study in literature review. • Establish a logical relation with previous research. • Clearly state how the research will advance theory and/or practice. • Clearly state the purpose as derived from the problem.
Method	• Have you provided general information describing what you did? • Have you provided specific information needed to facilitate replication and generalization?	• Describe participants in sufficient detail to facilitate generalization/replication. • Describe procedures in sufficient detail to facilitate generalization/replication. • Describe data collection procedures and measures in detail. • Describe technical adequacy of data collection measures, including those "home-grown." • Describe data analyses procedures.

Results	• Are results organized to facilitate understanding? • Are results presented with sufficient detail to foster confidence? • Have you considered practical significance of outcomes?	• Relate outcomes directly to implied or stated purpose (s) of the research. • Report outcomes using clarity and parsimony. • Use tables and figures appropriately and judiciously. • Provide sufficient information when reporting inferential statistics.
Discussion	• What are two or three key points that your work adds to the literature in special education? • What are the practical implications of your work? • What qualifying factors or limitations are appropriate?	• Derive important conclusions from outcomes of research. • Identify and consider alternative, rival hypotheses. • Link outcomes and conclusions to previous research findings. • Provide sufficient evidence to support conclusions. • Clearly describe implications for the improvement of practice.

Appendix H
Reporting Research Results

Standards for reporting results of specific types of studies have emerged over the years. With the increasing emphasis on evidence-based practice, it is especially important to adhere to the current, state-of-the-art reporting practices. Full and accurate reporting helps the research consumer evaluate the findings and their applicability to practice in other contexts. Including the relevant details also supports further research in the field, as scholars who develop studies often begin where others left off. Finally, providing sufficient information also makes a study more likely to be included in secondary analyses of research, such as meta-analyses and systematic literature reviews.

The Appendix to the APA *Publication Manual* (APA, 2010) contains helpful lists of content to report in all sections of the manuscript. Some specific suggestions are provided for experimental and quasi-experimental studies as well as meta-analyses (see pp. 247-253).

The following highlights several recommendations for what to report about study findings. Because different designs have different purposes and epistemological foundations, the sections are organized by broad design category. Recommendations are drawn from a variety of sources, including a series of articles published in two educational journals with detailed discussions of best practice for specific designs (Volume 71 Number 2 in *Exceptional Children* and Volumes 23-24 in *Journal of Early Intervention*).

Quantitative Designs

Group designs. Taxonomies for describing quantitative group designs vary, but they include descriptive, nonexperimental (i.e., correlational, causal-comparative, preexperimental), and experimental (i.e., true experimental and quasi-experimental) designs. The APA *Publication Manual* (APA, 2010, pp. 116-117) offers guidance for reporting statistics that are appropriate regardless of the design family. Sections 4.41 – 4.48 of the APA *Publication Manual* provide concrete guidance on conventional reporting practices and formats that should be followed for all quantitative group designs. Based on the APA *Publication*

Manual and several other publications, the following recommendations are offered:

1. Always include appropriate descriptive statistics, disaggregated by subgroups where appropriate.

2. Make efficient use of tables and figures, and attend to the correspondence of tables, figures, and text.

3. Provide full results of inferential statistics, for tests that were statistically significant as well as those that were not. Do not overinterpret the results (e.g., a test that yielded $p = .06$ is not "approaching" statistical significance).

4. Report and interpret confidence intervals.

5. Report and interpret effect size measures. Effects should be interpreted relative to what was found in similar research on the topic, or to standard statistical texts (e.g., Cohen, 1988), if no field-specific comparisons are available. See Trusty, Thompson, and Petrocelli (2004) for more guidance.

6. Interpret effect sizes in terms of practical significance, and inferential tests in terms of statistical significance.

The What Works Clearinghouse (WWC; http://ies.ed.gov/ncee/wwc/) is another driving source behind standards for reporting on experimental and quasiexperimental designs. The WWC (2008) uses several other types of information to decide whether a study is included in its meta-analyses, including

- The use of randomization and, as needed, evidence of group equivalence preintervention.

- Overall and differential attrition.

- Evidence for reliability and validity of measures.

- Confounding factors that may limit causal attribution.

For more detailed recommendations about specific quantitative designs, please see Gersten et al. (2005); Snyder (2000); or Thompson, Diamond, McWilliam, Snyder, and Snyder (2005).

Of course, best practices in reporting quantitative designs and results should also be preceded by the use of effective methods. Sources such as Osborne (2008) are helpful in guiding decisions about quantitative data analysis.

Single-subject designs. Although single-subject designs are experimental in nature, they use a very different set of statistics and reporting practices than group design research–in part because the individual is the unit of analysis. There are several reporting recommendations for these types of designs:

1. Describe the participants with detailed information, especially regarding characteristics that are germane to the intervention. This level of detail allows the reader to evaluate generalizability.

2. Provide detailed information about dependent variables, including how they were operationally defined and measured, their technical adequacy (e.g., interobserver agreement), and the frequency and duration of data collection during each phase of the study (i.e., baseline, intervention, alternate treatment, generalization).

3. Offer a description of the intervention that is sufficiently detailed to allow for replication. Also provide evidence of fidelity of implementation.

4. Use visual displays to convey the results. Follow conventions in the field for how to display results for different types of single-subject designs (e.g., alternating treatments, multiple baseline).

5. Interpret trends carefully in light of variability in the data. Although some effect size measures do exist for single-subject designs, their utility has recently been questioned (see Wolery, Busick, Reichow, & Barton, 2010).

For detailed recommendations on reporting in single-subject designs, consult Horner et al. (2005) or Wolery & Dunlap (2001).

Qualitative Designs

Unlike quantitative designs, qualitative research does not have highly defined, discrete criteria for reporting. There are also differences of opinion about how qualitative studies should be written and what constitutes evidence of "good" research. Whether qualitative research is written to adhere to the typical, 4-section outline seen in quantitative studies or follows a different narrative structure, is generally dependent upon the journal. However, regardless of perspective or structure, qualitative findings should be reported in such a way as to convince the reader of their trustworthiness. We offer several suggestions:

1. Make explicit links between direct evidence (i.e., data) and interpretation. Interpretations should be clearly grounded in the data to avoid the appearance of baseless opinions. Descriptions should be detailed.

2. Describe the theoretical framework(s) which guided interpretation.

3. Explain the researcher's role in the setting that was studied and his/her experience with the phenomenon.

4. Describe the methodological features that promote trustworthiness, such as the use of triangulation, member checking, memoing, verbatim transcripts, peer audits, persistent observation, negative case analysis, and/or prolonged engagement. How convinced was the researcher that saturation had been reached? Not all studies will use all of these strategies.

5. Be explicit in describing the steps in data analysis. It is insufficient to say data were "coded for emerging themes." What was the sequence of steps? What decisions did the researcher make about each step, and why? The authors' use of recursive data analysis techniques should be clear. If analytic techniques were drawn from other studies, reference those sources and explain what was adapted.

6. In journals with a more positivist orientation, reviewers may also look for evidence of dependability, such as interrater agreement on codes or adherence to a data collection protocol.

There is considerable diversity in qualitative designs, and the researcher's theoretical perspective will play a significant role in his or her approach to reporting findings. Readers are encouraged to consult Brantlinger, Jimenez, Klingner, Pugach, and Richardson (2005); Choudhuri, Glauser, and Peregoy (2004); or McWilliam (2000) for a more detailed discussion of qualitative designs, perspectives, and reporting practices.

Mixed Method Designs

Studies that combine quantitative and qualitative methods into "mixed methods" designs are becoming more common in education. These designs involve more than simply reporting quantitative and qualitative components separately, following the criteria highlighted previously. Mixed methods studies require the meaningful integration of the quantitative and qualitative components at one or more points during the research process (i.e., data collection, analysis, and interpretation). An excellent overview of the theoretical and practical considerations for mixed methods designs is provided in Creswell, Clark, Gutmann, and Hanson (2003). Based on this source, the following reporting practices are recommended:

1. Follow existing reporting practices for quantitative and qualitative design components.

2. Describe the researchers' choices of options for mixing the methods in terms of implementation sequence, which data have priority, when integration occurs, and what theoretical perspectives underlie the combination of methods.

3. Provide a figure that illustrates the use of the components and their integration.

4. Acknowledge the study strengths and weaknesses that come from using this design.

Appendix H References

American Psychological Association. (2010). *Publication manual of the American Psychological Association* (6ᵗʰ ed.). Washington, DC: Author.

Brantlinger, E., Jimenez, R., Klingner, J., Pugach, M., & Richardson, V. (2005). Qualitative studies in special education. *Exceptional Children, 71,* 195-207.

Choudhuri, D., Glauser, A., & Peregoy, J. (2004). Guidelines for writing a qualitative manuscript for the *Journal of Counseling & Development. Journal of Counseling & Development, 82,* 443-446.

Cohen, J. (1988). *Statistical power analysis for the behavioral sciences* (2ⁿᵈ ed.). Mahwah, NJ: Lawrence Erlbaum.

Creswell, J. W., Clark, V. L. P., Gutmann, M. L., & Hanson, W. E. (2003). Advanced mixed method research designs. In A. Tashakkori & C. Teddlie (Eds.), *Handbook of mixed methods in social and behavioral research* (pp. 209-240). Thousand Oaks, CA: Sage.

Gersten, R., Fuchs, L. S., Compton, D., Coyne, M., Greenwood, C., & Innocenti, M. S. (2005). Quality indicators for group experimental and quasi-experimental research in special education. *Exceptional Children, 71,* 149-164.

Horner, R. H., Carr, E. G., Halle, J., McGee, G., Odom, S. & Wolery, M. (2005). The use of single-subject research to identify evidence-based practice in special education. *Exceptional Children, 71,* 165-179.

McWilliam, R. A. (2000). Author and reviewer guideline series: Reporting qualitative studies. *Journal of Early Intervention, 23,* 77-80.

Osborne, J. W. (Ed.). (2008). *Best practices in quantitative methods.* Thousand Oaks, CA: Sage.

Snyder, P. (2000). Guidelines for reporting results of group quantitative investigations. *Journal of Early Intervention, 23,* 145-150.

Thompson, B., Diamond, K. E., McWilliam, R., Snyder, P., & Snyder, S. W. (2005). Evaluating the quality of evidence from correlational research for evidence-based practice. *Exceptional Children, 71*, 181-194.

Trusty, J., Thompson, B., & Petrocelli, J. V. (2004). Practical guide for reporting effect size in quantitative research in the *Journal of Counseling & Development. Journal of Counseling & Development, 82,* 107-110.

What Works Clearinghouse. (2008, December). *WWC procedures and standards handbook, version 2.0.* Retrieved from http://ies.ed.gov/ncee/wwc/references/idocviewer/doc.aspx?docid=19&tocid=1

Wolery, M., Busick, M., Reichow, B., & Barton, E. E. (2010). Comparison of overlap methods for quantitatively synthesizing single-subject data. *The Journal of Special Education, 44,* 18-28.

Wolery, M., & Dunlap, G. (2001). Reporting on studies using single-subject experimental methods. *Journal of Early Intervention, 24,* 85-89.

Appendix I
Tips for Moving From the 5ᵗʰ to the 6ᵗʰ Edition

Text Tips (APA, 2010, pp. 62-63)

- Use boldface print for major sections of the manuscript (**Method**, **Results**, **Discussion**), centered headings; [other centered headings (Abstract and References) are not bolded.]

- Use boldface print for headings that were italicized in the 5ᵗʰ ed. (e.g., flush-left heading, paragraph heading)

General Tips (APA, 2010, pp. 87-88)

- Use a single space after punctuation marks in text, reference citations, and initials in names.

Reference List Tips for Articles With Digital Object Identifier (APA, 2010, p. 198-199)

- Use digital object identifier (DOI) code, if one has been assigned.

Example of DOI for Published Article With From One to Seven Authors

Spooner, F., Algozzine, B., Wood, C. L., & Hicks, S. C. (2010). What we know and need to know about teacher education and special education. *Teacher Education and Special Education, 33,* 44-54. doi: 10.1177/0888406409356184

Example of DOI for Article with More than Seven Authors

Author, A., Author, B., Author, C., Author, D., Author, E., Author, F., . . . Author, J. (date). Title of article. *Journal Title, xx,* pp-pp. doi: xx.xxxxxxxxxx

Example of DOI for Advance Online Publication

Test, D. W., Richter, S., Knight, V., & Spooner, F. (2010). A comprehensive review and meta-analysis of the social stories literature. *Focus on Autism and Other Developmental Disabilities.* Advance online publication. doi: 10.1177/1088357609351573

Source. Adapted from American Psychological Association (APA). (2010). *Publication manual of the American Psychological Association* (6ᵗʰ ed.). Washington, DC: Author.